CHINESE
STEP-BY-STEP

STEP ONE

FOREWORD

Students of Chinese as a second language consider the writing and retention of characters and their pronunciation, especially the needed practice and drill in the four tone changes, difficult and boring. **Chinese Step-by-Step, Step One** has been designed to improve upon this problem -- the text introduces the characters while teaching their pronunciation. Students will be able to recognize the sound and correct stroke order for each character used in pronunciation practice drills and apply this knowledge to the formation of new words. The text motivates students to reach a goal of willingly participating in repeated pronunciation drill practice to the extent that words and phrases learned are actively used in communicative sentences leading to the development of simple daily conversation.

The first seven units introduce the character and pictorial representations for one hundred fairly common concrete nouns; there are no abstract concepts in these units. For example 窩 窝 (WŌ; ㄨㄛ) is a concrete noun meaning "nest". It's purpose is to drill the pronunciation of the "wu" (ㄨ) sound. Later, after the character 鳥 鸟 (NIĂO; ㄋㄧㄠ) is learned, students will learn "bird nest" 鳥窩; 鸟窝 (NIĂO WŌ; ㄋㄧㄠ ㄨㄛ) by combining the two characters together. Even more, by switching the two characters and by placing the number "one" in front of it, a new phrase meaning "a nest of birds" is formed. Afterwards, when students learn the word for "dog", it is possible to make the phrase "a den of dogs". Another example is 蕊 蕊 pistil. Everyone thinks that since this character does not appear frequently, why bother to study it? It is studied because the "R" sound in Chinese is very difficult to pronounce. Four characters 日 (sun), 人 (people), 肉 (meat), and 蕊 蕊 (pistil) are introduced for practice with the "R" sound. 日, 人, and 肉 are all useful and common, but 蕊 蕊 serves a special purpose: to represent the sound "RUI". The form of this character is very interesting -- three 心 's (heart) under a plant radical means the pistil is the heart of the flower -- it will help students to understand the composition of characters and remember pronunciations.

Each Chinese character has two parts: the "initial" (consonant) and the "final" (vowel), and is pronounced monosyllabically. **Chinese Step-by-Step, Step One** emphasizes the 21 initial consonants and only four of the 16 vowels -- YI, WU, YU, ER. (Vowels will be emphasized in **Step Two**.) Four characters are selected to drill each of these twenty-five sounds (100 characters in all). For example: (ZHI; ㄓ) sound uses 竹 bamboo (ZHÚ; ㄓㄨˊ) 豬 猪 (ZHŪ; ㄓㄨ) pig, 桌 (ZHUŌ; ㄓㄨㄛ) table, 紙 纸 (ZHĬ; ㄓˇ) paper. In introducing the sound of (ZHI; ㄓ) bamboo 竹 is used as the model sound; students learn its phonetic transcription and its stroke order. Bamboo was picked because it is simple, it's a radical or root of Chinese characters and uses only six strokes. The other three characters are interesting, practical and a knowledge of them could motivate a student to generate and make use of other words that can be utilized creatively in conversations, reading and writing.

This book includes two phonetic systems. One is the Pinyin system from Beijing, China, and the other is the BoPoMoFo (ㄅ, ㄆ, ㄇ, ㄈ) system from Taiwan. Simplified characters, promoted officially by the Beijing government of China, are also included.

Chinese: Step-by-Step, Step One focuses on Traditional characters and the Pinyin phonetic system. Simplified characters and BoPoMoFo phonetic symbols serve as a reference.

Gwen T. Wang

謝桐支

note dragon & phoenix on cover!

CHINESE
STEP-BY-STEP
中文入門

STEP ONE
第一步

Gwen T. Wang

著作者:謝桐光

Addison-Wesley Publishing Company, Inc.
Reading, Massachusetts • Menlo Park, California
Don Mills, Ontario • Wokingham, England • Amsterdam • Sydney
Singapore • Tokyo • Mexico City • Bogota • Santiago • San Juan

The author and the publisher wish to thank:

Carol P. Chen, ESOL and Chinese Teacher
Montgomery Public Schools, Maryland

Dr. Adele Rickett, Chairperson
Hebrew and Eastern Language Department
University of Maryland
College Park, Maryland

Brenda Lansdown, formerly at Brooklyn College
Currently working in the field of experimental
education in China

Illustrator: Yan-Yu Tse

插圖:謝雁羽

A publication of the World Language Division

Janet H. Muller, Production Coordinator
James W. Gibbons, Production/Manufacturing

ISBN: 0-201-09604-8
ABCDEFGHIJ-AL-898765

Contents

UNIT 1
1

Initial Sounds

衣
clothes
屋
room
雨
rain

UNIT 2
11

Initial Sounds

竹
bamboo
尺
ruler
水
water
日
sun

UNIT 3
23

Initial Sounds

子
seed
刺
thorn
松
pine

UNIT 4
35

Initial Sounds

杯
cup
皮
skin
毛
fur
房
house

UNIT 5
47

Initial Sounds

刀
knife
田
field
牛
cow
李
plum

UNIT 6
61

Initial Sounds

果
fruit
口
opening
火
fire

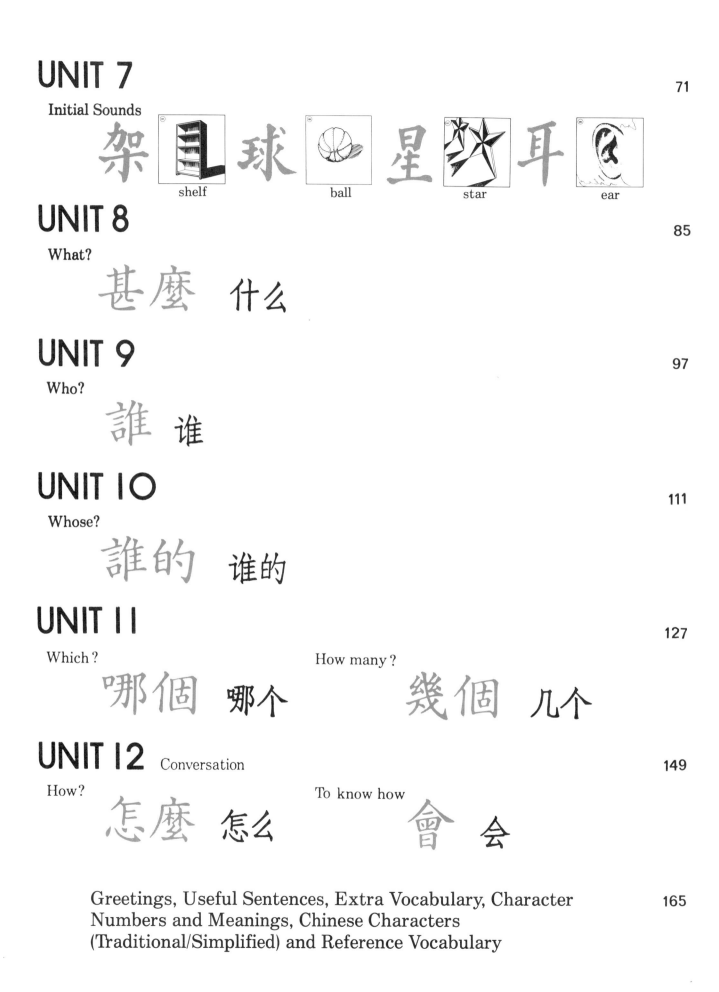

Pronunciation Guide

The Four Tones

Symbols	Pronunciation Key	Examples
1st tone	HIGH AND EVEN sing as – 🎼	YĪ; ㄧ MĀO; ㄇㄠ
2nd tone	FROM LOW TO HIGH say as – ME? ↗	YÚ; ㄩˊ MÁO; ㄇㄠˊ
3rd tone	DOWN AND UP say as – WELL?	YǏ; ㄧˇ SHǓ; ㄕㄨˇ
4th tone	FROM HIGH TO LOW say as – HI! ↘	YÙ; ㄩˋ SHÙ; ㄕㄨˋ

Note: The mark for the lst tone in the Pinyin system is different from the mark in the BoPoMoFo system. e.g., in the Pinyin MĀO there is an accent on the top of the vowel. In BoPoMoFo ㄇㄠ no accent is used.

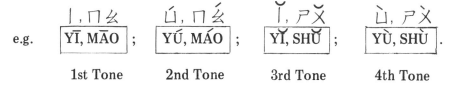

ㄧ, ㄇㄠ	ㄩˊ, ㄇㄠˊ	ㄧˇ, ㄕㄨˇ	ㄩˋ, ㄕㄨˋ
e.g. YĪ, MĀO ;	YÚ, MÁO ;	YǏ, SHǓ ;	YÙ, SHÙ .
1st Tone	2nd Tone	3rd Tone	4th Tone

UNIT I

Initial Sounds

    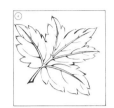

ORAL DRILL

1. The four tones

1st Tone	2nd Tone	3rd Tone	4th Tone

Figure showing the four tones.

- ⑤ High-pitch
- ④ Mid-high-pitch
- ③ Middle-pitch
- ② Mid-low-pitch
- ① Low-pitch

Each sound has four tones. Throughout the book, practice each sound using the four tones.

e.g.

YĪ	YÍ	YǏ	YÌ
clothes		chair	
WŪ	WÚ	WǓ	WÙ
room			
YŪ	YÚ	YǓ	YÙ
	fish	rain	jade

2. The numbers one (1) and five (5).

YĪ WǓ

1

Pronunciation Guide

Shape of the lips	Phonetic Symbols		Pronounce like
	PINYIN	BOPOMOFO	
Open your mouth, flatten your lips and say "ee".	YI (y–; –i)	─ ⟶	S<u>EE</u>
Round your lips into a small circle and say "oo".	WU (w–; –u)	ㄨ ㄨˊ	P<u>OO</u>L
Round your lips into a small circle and say "ee".	YU (yu–; –ü)	ㄩ ㄩˊ	The French "*ü*"
Open your mouth wide and say "ah".	A	ㄚ ㄚˊ	F<u>A</u>THER
Open your mouth, round your lips and say "aw".	O	ㄛ ㄛˊ	S<u>A</u>W
Open your mouth, flatten your lips and say "er".	E	ㄜ ㄜˊ	H<u>E</u>R
Open your mouth, flatten your lips and say "ey".	E	ㄝ ㄝˊ	Y<u>E</u>T H<u>EY</u>

Notes:

1. There are 3 written forms for "YI, WU, YU" in the Pinyin system.

    YI, WU, YU as independent sounds
        e.g., Y<u>Ī</u>; W<u>Ū</u>; Y<u>Ū</u>

    Y-, W-, YU- as initial sounds
        e.g., Y<u>Ā</u>N; W<u>Ā</u>N; YU<u>Ā</u>N

    -i; -u; -ü   as final sounds
        e.g., L<u>Ǐ</u>; L<u>Ǔ</u>; L<u>Ǚ</u>

2. In writing all phonetic symbols in the BOPOMOFO system, do not exceed 3 strokes. e.g., ㄚ=3 strokes; ㄛ =2 strokes.

clothes

Match each picture with the correct character from pages 9 and 10.

5

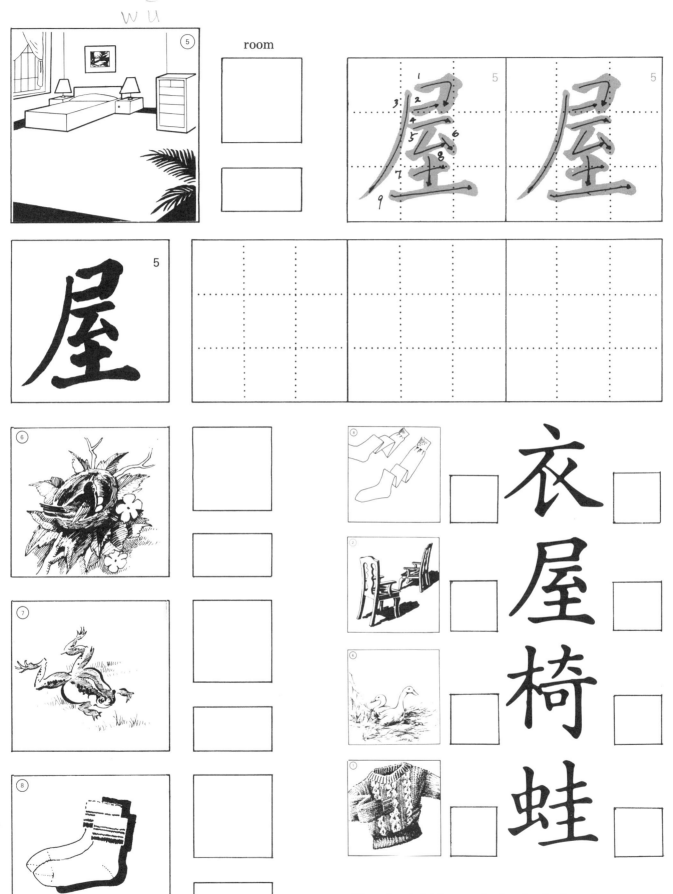

room

Give the initial sounds for both the pictures and the characters.

yǔ

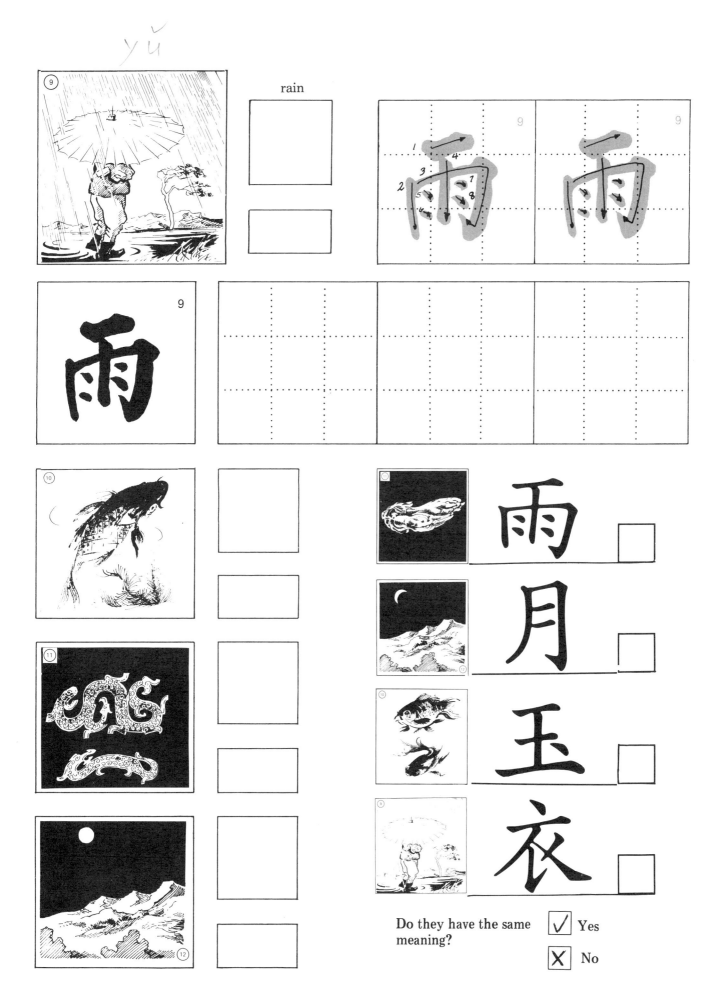

rain

Do they have the same meaning?

☑ Yes

☒ No

Pronunciation Drill

Practice the tones.
(Identify the pictures with phonetic transcriptions.)

1st tone

 2nd tone

 3rd tone

 4th tone

Flashcards

衣 (1)	蛙 (7)	玉 (11)
鴨 (3)	魚 (10)	月 (12)
屋 (5)	雨 (9)	葉 (4)
窩 (6)	椅 (2)	襪 (8)

衣
衣
椅
椅
鴨
鴨
葉
葉
屋
窩
蛙
襪

月	玉	魚	雨

Flashcards

衣
衣
椅
椅
鸭
鸭
叶
叶
屋
窝
蛙
袜

玉 11	蛙 7	衣 1
月 12	鱼 10	鸭 3
叶 4	雨 9	屋 5
袜 8	椅 2	窝 6

雨	鱼	玉	月

UNIT 2

Initial Sounds

ORAL DRILL

1. I'm a teacher, and you?   WǑ SHÌ LǍO SHĪ, NǏ NE?

2. What's this?   ZHÈ SHÌ SHÉNME?

   This is _____.   ZHÈ SHÌ _____.

3. I don't know.   WǑ BÙ ZHĪ DAO.

4. The same, not the same   YÍ YÀNG, BÙ YÍ YÀNG

5. The number (10)   SHÍ

11

Pronunciation Guide

Phonetic Symbols		Pronunciation Key
PINYIN	**BOPOMOFO**	**Put the tip of your tongue against the roof of your mouth and say-**
ZHI (zh-)	业 业	"**j**" as in **j**erk
CHI (ch-)	彳 彳	"**ch**" as in **ch**ur**ch**
SHI (sh-)	尸 尸	"**sh**" as in **sh**irt
RI (r-)	日 日	"**r**" as in **r**ubber
ANG	尢 尢	"**ong**" as in g**ong**"
EN	ㄣ ㄣ	"**un**" as in r**un**
OU	又 又	say "**oe**" as in h**oe**
EI	ㄟ ㄟ	say "**ei**" as in **ei**ght

Notes:

The sound "i" never occurs after "ZH", "CH", "SH", or "R" in the Peking dialect. Therefore in words spelled "ZHI", "CHI", "SHI", and "RI", the "i's" are silent.

ZH-; CH-; SH-, R- as initial sounds
 e.g. ZHŪ; CHĒ; SHUĬ; RÒU

bamboo

Match the picture with the correct character. (Use the characters on pages 21 and 22.)

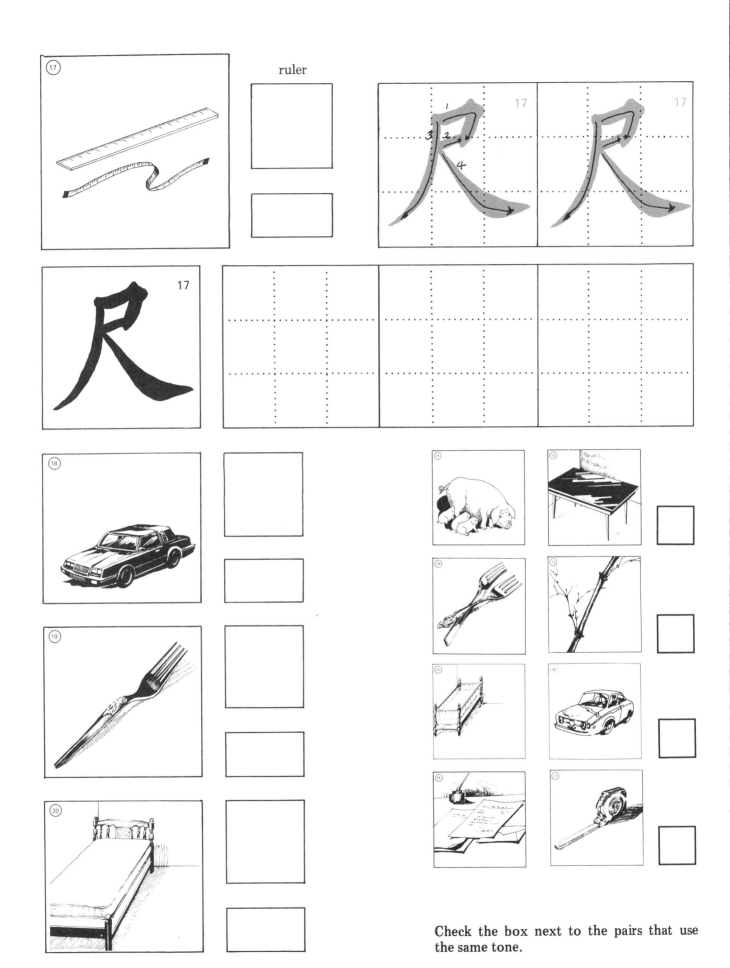

ruler

Check the box next to the pairs that use the same tone.

water

水

Name the objects you know in this picture.

19

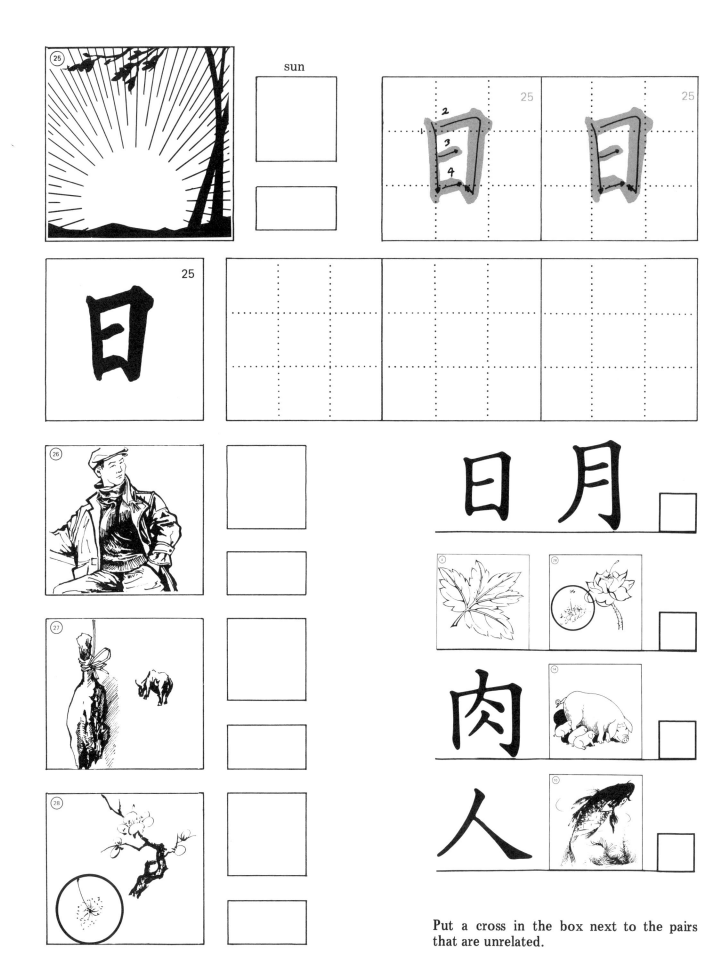

sun

日

Put a cross in the box next to the pairs that are unrelated.

Flashcards

車 [18]	桌 [15]	叉 [19]
人 [26]	竹 [13]	牀 [20]
尺 [17]	紙 [16]	水 [21]
鼠 [22]	日 [25]	慈 [28]

竹
竹
豬
豬
桌
桌
紙
紙
尺
車
叉
牀

慈	肉	人	日	樹	書	鼠	水

Flashcards

竹	叉 19	桌 15	车 18
竹	床 20	竹 13	人 26
猪	水 21	纸 16	尺 17
猪	蕊 28	日 25	鼠 22
桌			
桌			
纸			
纸			
尺			
车			
叉			
床	水	鼠	书	树	日	人	肉	蕊

UNIT 3

Initial Sounds

   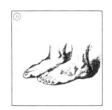 

    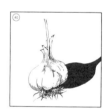

ORAL DRILL

1. What's this?   ZHÈ SHÌ SHÉNME?

2. (It's) here.   ZÀI.

3. The expressions:
   How do you do?   NǏ HǍO?
   Good morning   ZǍO
   once more   ZÀI YÍ CÌ
   Good bye   ZÀI JIÀN

4. The numbers three (3) and four (4)   SĀN, SÌ

5. The colors - purple and brown   ZǏ, ZŌNG

Pronunciation Guide

Phonetic Symbols		Pronunciation Key
PINYIN	BOPOMOFO	
Z (z-)	ㄗ ㄗ	say "**ds**" as in **reads**
C (c-)	ㄘ ㄘ	say "**ts**" as in **its**
S (s-)	ㄙ ㄙ	say "**s**" as in "**sit**"
AI	ㄞ ㄞ	say "**eye**"
AN	ㄢ ㄢ	say "**an**" as in **fiance**
AO	ㄠ ㄠ	say "**ow**" as in **now**
ENG	ㄥ ㄥ	say "**ung**" as in **sung**
ONG	ㄨㄥ	say "**won**" as in **won**'t
UAN	ㄨㄢ	say "**one**"
UI	ㄨㄟ	say "**way**"

Notes:

To pronounce "Z", "C", and "S" place the tip of the tongue behind your upper teeth. Pronounce these sounds as "ZH", "CH", and "SH" without curling your tongue.

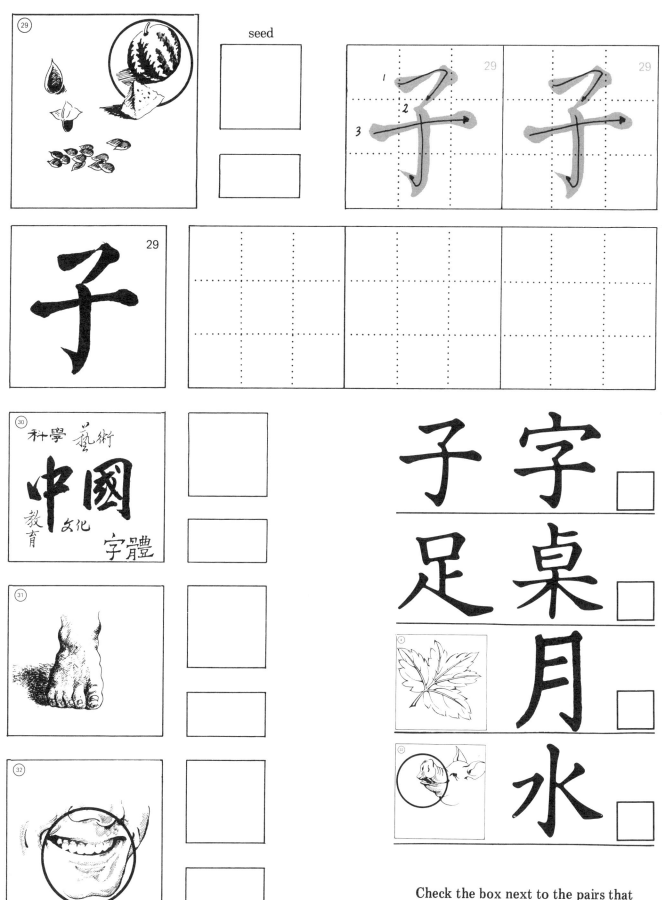

seed

子

子

Check the box next to the pairs that rhyme.

thorn

Check the box next to the pairs that use the same tone.

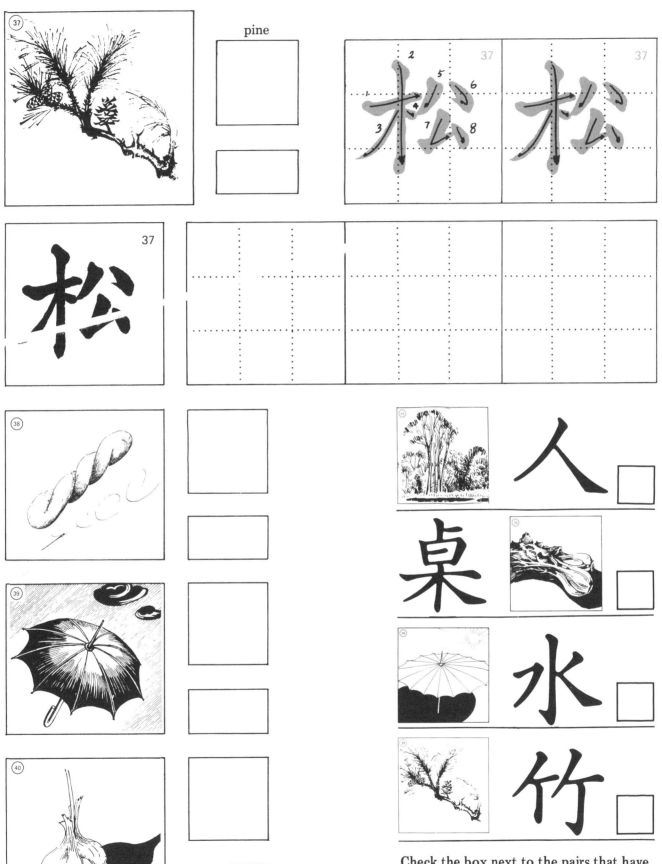

pine

Check the box next to the pairs that have the some connection. Explain your answer.

Compound Nouns

NOUN + NOUN = COMPOUND NOUN · MEANING

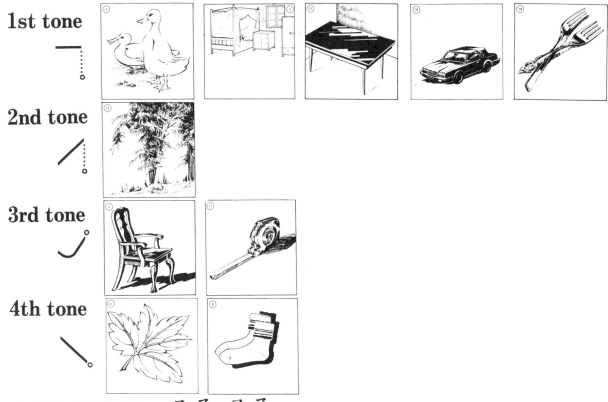

COMPOUND NOUN	MEANING
雨 衣	raincoat
蛙 人	frogman
___ 肉	pork

NOUNS ENDING IN 子 *

1st tone

2nd tone

3rd tone

4th tone

* NOMINAL SUFFIX i.e., 尺子, 叉子 etc.

The nominal suffix 子 is usually pronounced weak and short. When it is used in a 3rd tone prefix the 子 is pronounced high and short.

Flashcards

蔥 36	松 37	絲 38
子 29	嘴 32	足 31
傘 39	草 35	字 30
蒜 40	菜 34	刺 33

子
字
足
嘴
刺
菜
草
蔥
松
絲
傘
蒜

Flashcards

子		
字	丝 38	松 37	葱 36
足		
咀	足 31	咀 32	子 29
刺		
菜	字 30	草 35	伞 39
草		
葱	刺 33	菜 34	蒜 40
松		
丝		
伞		
蒜		

EVALUATION 1

Read aloud.

1st tone

衣　鴨　屋　窩　蛙

豬　桌　車　叉　書

蔥　松　絲

2nd tone

魚　竹　牀　人　足

3rd tone

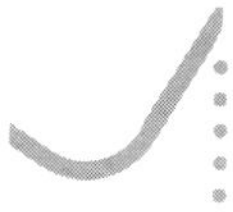

椅　雨　紙　尺　水

鼠　蕊　子　嘴　草　傘

4th tone

葉　襪　玉　月　樹

日　肉　字　刺　菜　蒜

EVALUATION 1

Read aloud.

					1st tone
蛙 7	窝 6	屋 5	鸭 3	衣 1	
书 23	叉 19	车 18	桌 15	猪 14	
		丝 38	松 37	葱 36	

					2nd tone
足 31	人 26	床 20	竹 13	鱼 10	

					3rd tone
水 21	尺 17	纸 16	雨 9	椅 2	
伞 39	草 35	咀 32	子 29	蕊 28	鼠 22

					4th tone
树 24	月 12	玉 11	袜 8	叶 4	
蒜 40	莱 34	刺 33	字 30	肉 27	日 25

Initial Sounds

   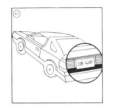 

ORAL DRILL (– MA?)

MĀ	MÁ	MǍ	MÀ	MA	MĀMA MÀ MǍ MA?
mom	hemp	horse	scold	question mark	

1. Is this _____ ?   ZHÈ SHÌ _____ MA?

2. Are you _____ ?   NǏ SHÌ _____ MA?

3. It's not here.   BÚ ZÀI.

4. The number 8   BĀ

5. The color white   BÁI

35

Pronunciation Drill

Phonetic Symbols		Pronunciation Key
PINYIN	BOPOMOFO	
B	ㄅ ㄅ	say "**b**" as in **b**all
P	ㄆ ㄆ	say "**p**" as in **p**op
M	ㄇ ㄇ	say "**m**" as in **m**ore
F	ㄈ ㄈ	say "**f**" as in **f**ork
ANG	ㄤ ㄤ	"**ong**" as in g**ong**"
ENG	ㄥ	say "**ung**" as in s**ung**
ING	ㄥ	say "**ing**" as in s**ing**

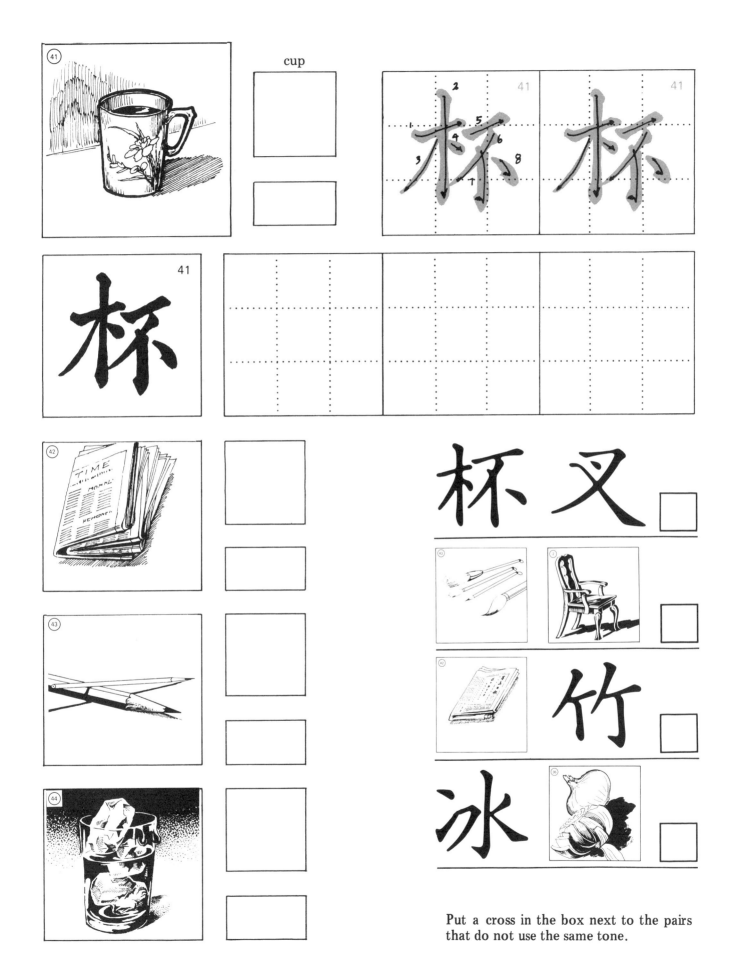

cup

Put a cross in the box next to the pairs that do not use the same tone.

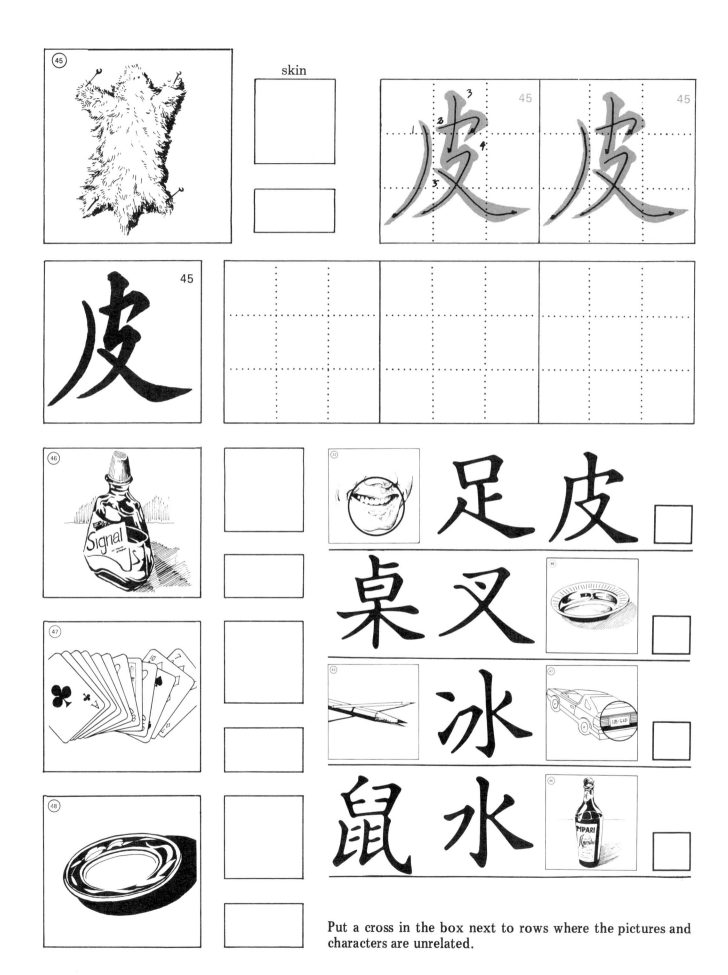

skin

Put a cross in the box next to rows where the pictures and characters are unrelated.

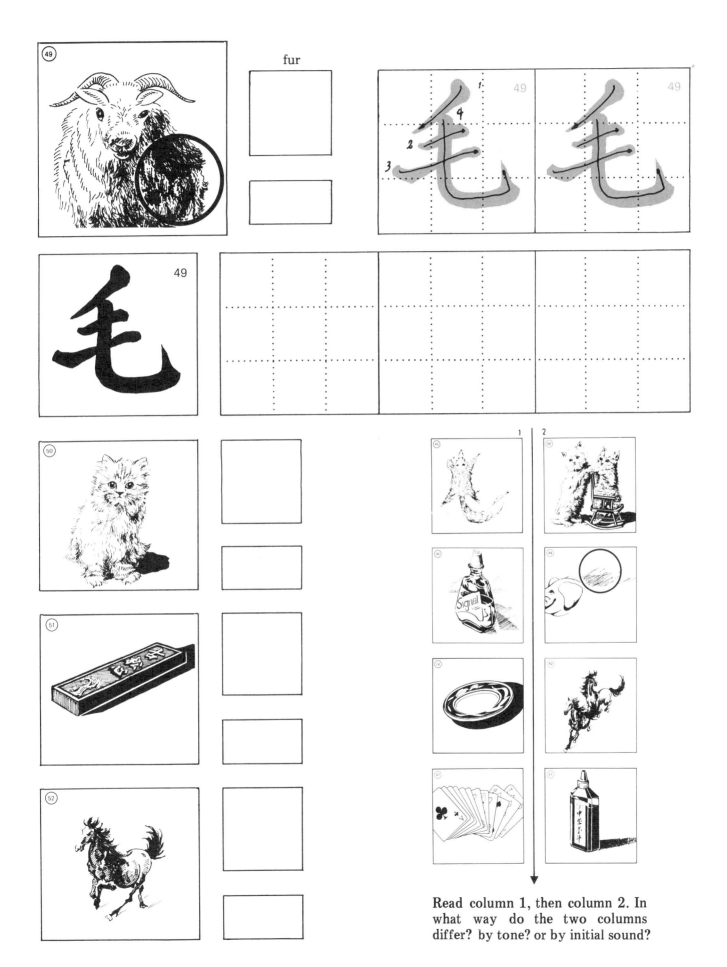

fur

Read column 1, then column 2. In what way do the two columns differ? by tone? or by initial sound?

house

房

Draw a straight line through the three connecting characters and pictures that have the same tone.

Flashcards

杯 **41**	冰 **44**	皮 **45**
髮 **56**	墨 **51**	瓶 **46**
馬 **52**	筆 **43**	牌 **47**
房 **53**	毛 **49**	盤 **48**

杯
報
筆
冰
皮
瓶
牌
盤
毛
貓
墨
馬

髮	鳳	風	房

Flashcards

杯
报
笔
冰
皮
瓶
牌
盘
毛
猫
墨
马

皮 45	冰 44	杯 41
瓶 46	墨 51	发 56
牌 47	笔 43	马 52
盘 48	毛 49	房 53

房	风	凤	发

UNIT 5

Initial Sounds

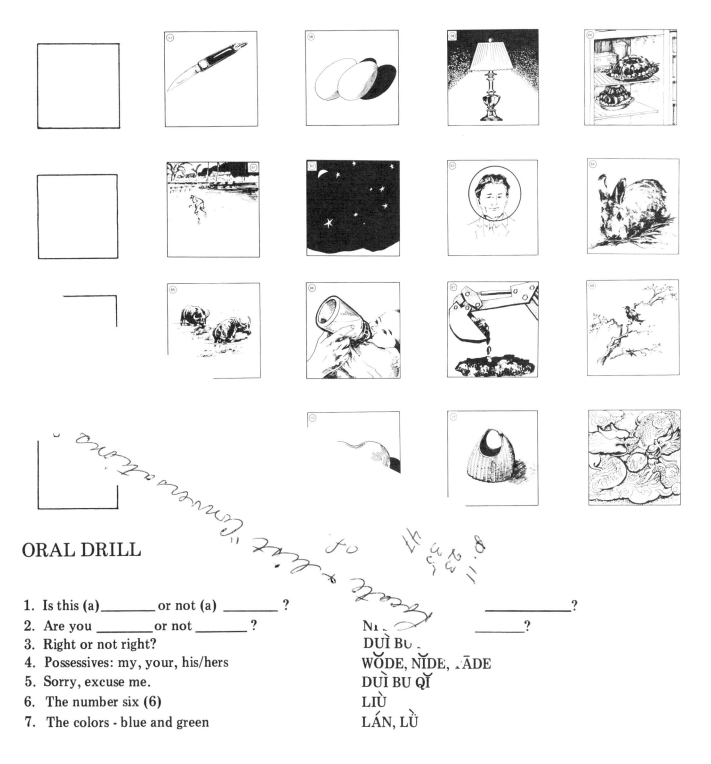

ORAL DRILL

1. Is this (a) _____ or not (a) _____ ?   _____ ?
2. Are you _____ or not _____ ?   Nı̆ ___   _____ ?
3. Right or not right?   DUÌ BU ___
4. Possessives: my, your, his/hers   WǑDE, NǏDE, TĀDE
5. Sorry, excuse me.   DUÌ BU QǏ
6. The number six (6)   LIÙ
7. The colors - blue and green   LÁN, LǛ

Pronunciation Guide

Phonetic Symbols		Pronunciation Key
PINYIN	BOPOMOFO	
D	ㄉ ㄉ	say "**d**" as in **d**ate
T	ㄊ ㄊ	say "**t**" as in **t**ell
N	ㄋ ㄋ	say "**n**" as in **n**ice
L	ㄌ ㄌ	say "**l**" as in **l**et
IAN	ㄧㄢ	say "**yen**"
IAO	ㄧㄠ	say "**yow**"
IU	ㄧㄡ	say "**yo**" as in **yo**ke

Flashcards

49

天 TIAN	ㄊㄢ 天 62

燈 DĒNG	ㄉㄥ 灯 59

刀 DĀO	ㄉㄠ 刀 57

鳥 NIǍO	ㄋㄧㄠ 鸟 68

李 LǏ	ㄌㄧ 李 69

奶 NǍI	ㄋㄞ 奶 66

凍 DÒNG	ㄉㄨㄥ 冻 60

兔 TÙ	ㄊㄨ 兔 64

蛋 DÀN	ㄉㄢ 蛋 58

Flashcards

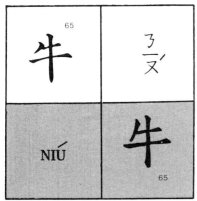

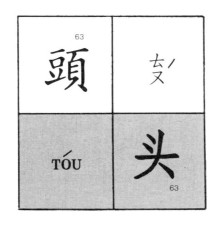

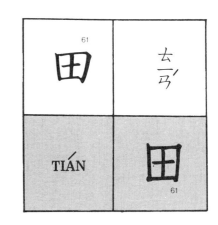

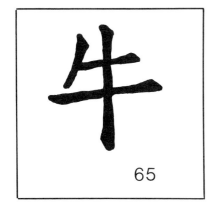

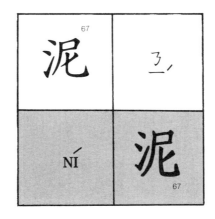

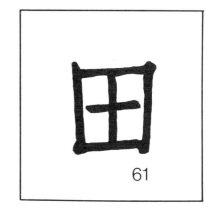

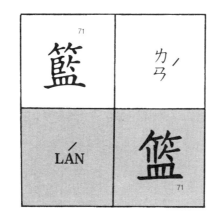

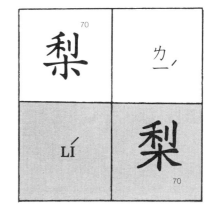

Flashcards

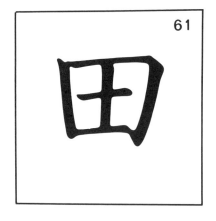

61

田

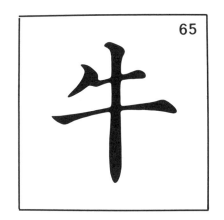

65

牛

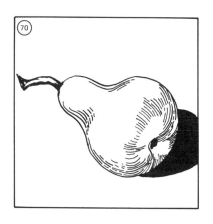

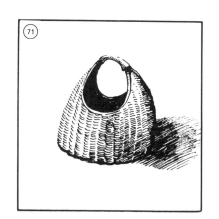

70

梨

71

籃

72

龍

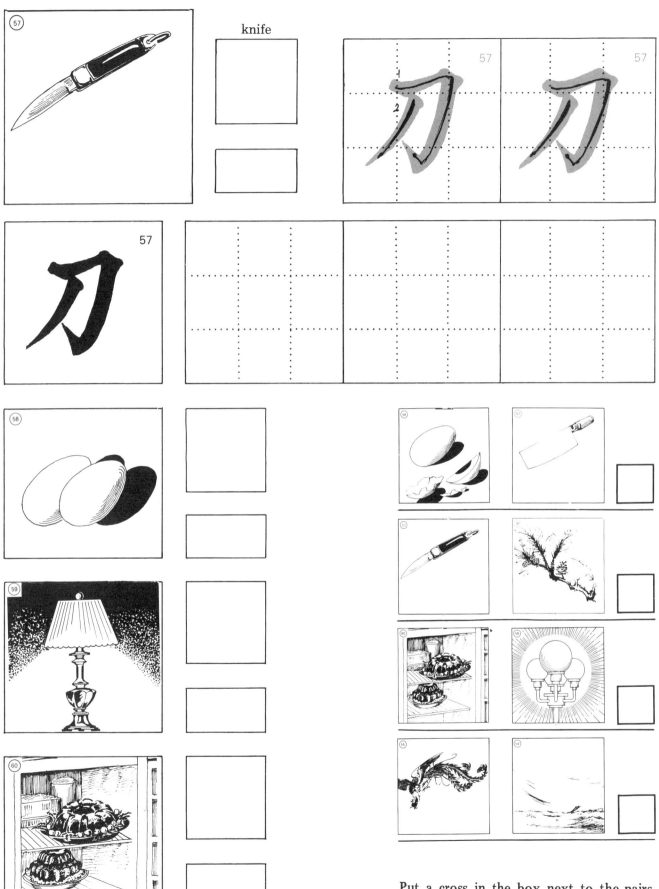

knife

Put a cross in the box next to the pairs that use the same tone.

field

Name the objects you know in this picture.

54

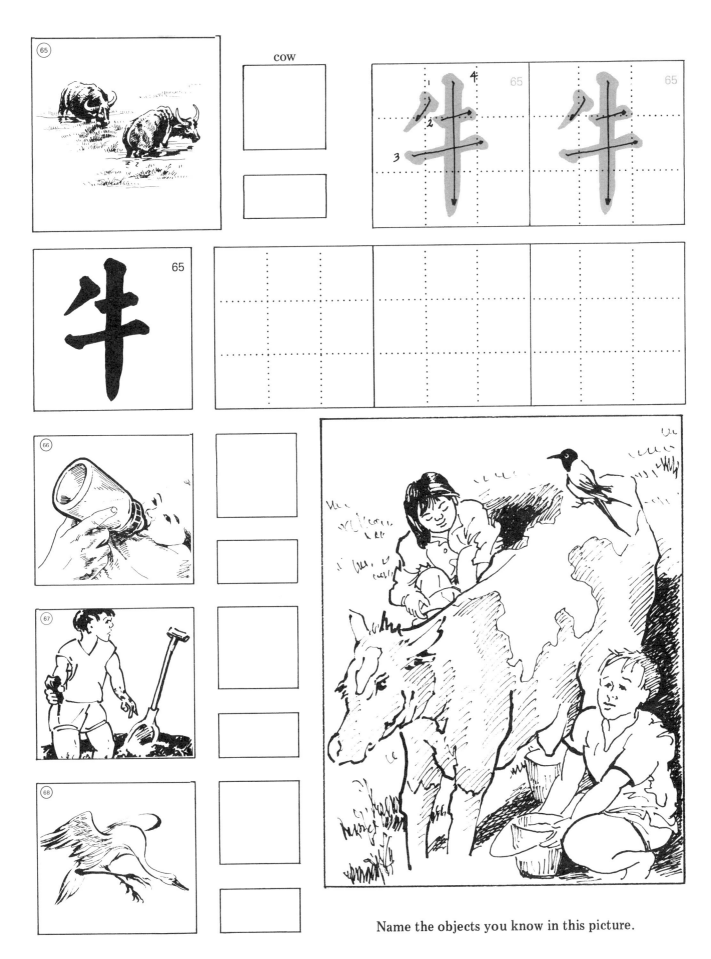

cow

Name the objects you know in this picture.

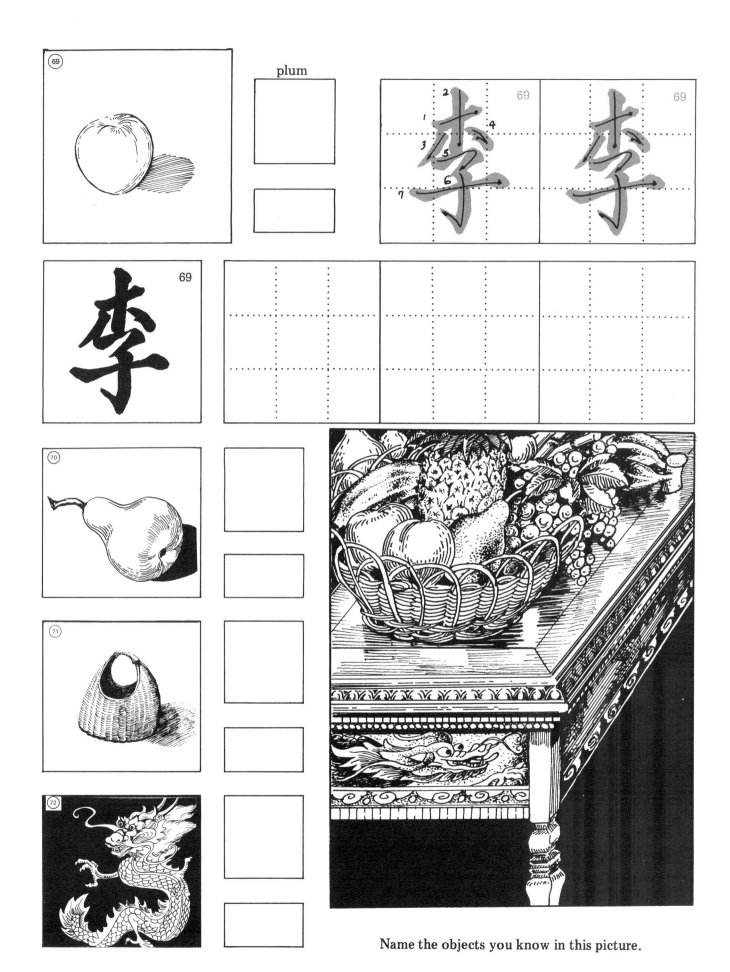

plum

Name the objects you know in this picture.

Flashcards

刀 57	燈 59	夭 62
鳥 68	奶 66	李 69
蛋 58	兔 64	凍 60
頭 63	泥 67	牛 65

龍	籃	梨	李

刀
蛋
燈
凍
田
夭
頭
兔
牛
奶
泥
鳥

Flashcards

刀			
蛋	天 62	灯 59	刀 57
灯			
冻	李 69	奶 66	鸟 68
田			
天			
头	冻 60	兔 64	蛋 58
兔			
牛	牛 65	泥 67	头 63
奶			
泥			

鸟	李	梨	篮	龙

EVALUATION 2

Phonetic Transcription		72 Chinese Characters			
		1st TONE	2nd TONE	3rd TONE	4th TONE
一	Y-	衣，鴨（鸭）		椅	葉（叶）
ㄨ	W-	屋,蛙,窩（窝）			襪（袜）
ㄩ	YU-		魚（鱼）	雨	玉，月
ㄓ	ZH-	豬（猪），桌 竹		紙（纸）	
ㄔ	CH-	車（车）叉	牀（床）	尺	
ㄕ	SH-	書（书）		水，鼠	樹（树）
ㄖ	R-		人	蕊（蕊）	日，肉
ㄗ	Z-		足	子,嘴（咀）	字
ㄘ	C-	葱（葱）		草（草）	刺，菜（菜）
ㄙ	S-	松，絲（丝）		傘（伞）	蒜（蒜）
ㄅ	B-	杯，冰		筆（笔）	報（报）
ㄆ	P-		皮,瓶,牌,盤（盘）		
ㄇ	M-	貓（猫）	毛	馬（马）	墨
ㄈ	F-	風（风）	房		鳳（凤）,髮（发）
ㄉ	D-	刀，燈（灯）			蛋，凍（冻）
ㄊ	T-	天	田，頭（头）		兔
ㄋ	N-		牛，泥	奶，鳥（鸟）	
ㄌ	L-		梨籃（篮）龍(龙)	李	

59

NOUN + NOUN = COMPOUND NOUN   MEANING

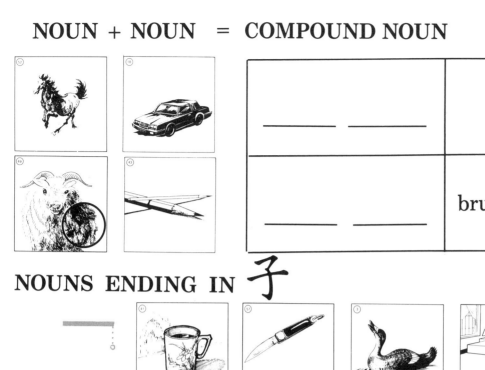

	carriage
_____ _____	
	brush pen (Chinese)
_____ _____	

NOUNS ENDING IN 子

   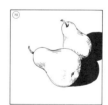 

60

UNIT 6

Initial Sounds

    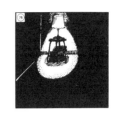

ORAL DRILL (HÁI SHÌ)

1. Expressions
   a. How are you?   NǏ HǍO MA?
      Very good.   HĚN HǍO
      Wonderful.   HǍO JÍ LE

   b. Congratulations.   GŌNGXI GŌNGXI
      Congratulations and be prosperous.   GŌNGXǏ FĀ CÁI
      Happy New Year.   GŌNG HÈ XĪN XǏ

2. a. Is this (a)_____ or (a) _____ ?   ZHÈ SHÌ____ HÁI SHÌ _____?
      It is (a) _____ .   ZHÈ SHÌ_____.

   b. Are you_____ or _____?   NǏ SHÌ_____ HÁI SHÌ _____?
      I am _____.   WǑ SHÌ_____.

   c. Is this ____ DE or _____DE?   ZHÈ SHÌ _____ DE HÁI SHÌ_____ DE?

3. The colors - red, yellow, black and gray   HÓNG, HUÁNG, HĒI, HUĪ.

Pronunciation Guide

Phonetic Symbols		Pronunciation Key
PINYIN	**BOPOMOFO**	
G	《 　 《²	say "**g**" as in **g**irl
K	ㄎ 　 ㄎ²	say "**k**" as in **K**urt
H	ㄏ 　 ㄏ²	say "**h**" as in **h**er
UA	ㄨㄚ	say "**ua**" as in sq**ua**sh
UAI	ㄨㄞ	say "**wi**" as in **wi**fe
UANG	ㄨㄤ	say "**wahng**"
UN	ㄨㄣ	say "**oo**" and "**en**" together quickly
UO	ㄨㄛ	say "**uaw**" as in sq**uaw**

82 猴 ㄏㄡˊ	HÓU 猴 82	76 光 ㄍㄨㄤ	GUĀNG 光 76	83 花 ㄏㄨㄚ	HUĀ 花 83
75 棍 ㄍㄨㄣˋ	GÙN 棍 75	73 果 ㄍㄨㄛˇ	GUǑ 果 73	74 狗 ㄍㄡˇ	GǑU 狗 74
80 褲 ㄎㄨˋ	KÙ 褲 80	77 口 ㄎㄡˇ	KǑU 口 77	81 火 ㄏㄨㄛˇ	HUǑ 火 81
79 筷 ㄎㄨㄞˋ	KUÀI 筷 79	78 釦 ㄎㄡˋ	KÒU 扣 78	84 畫 ㄏㄨㄚˋ	HUÀ 画 84

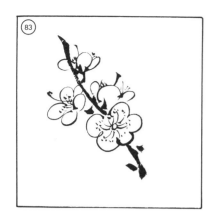

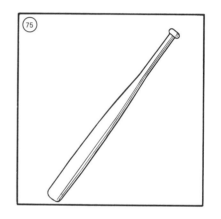

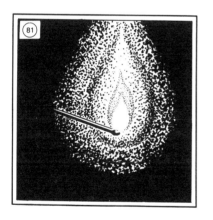

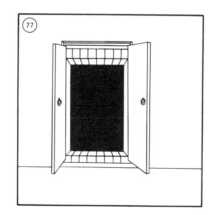

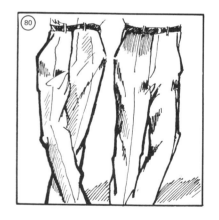

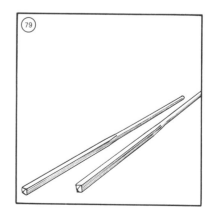

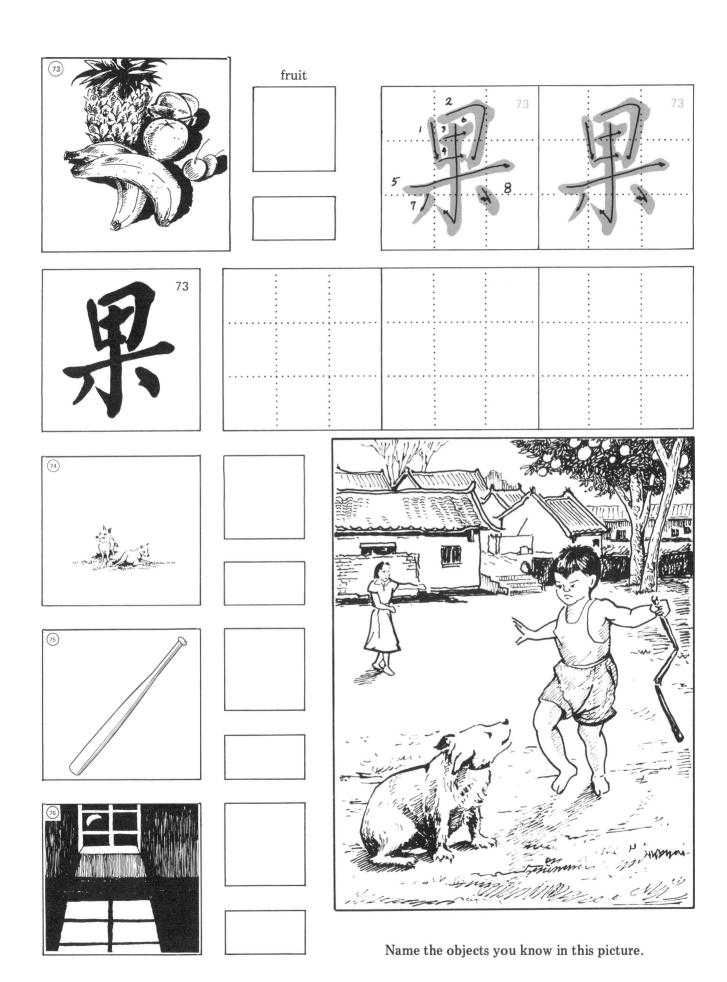

fruit

果

Name the objects you know in this picture.

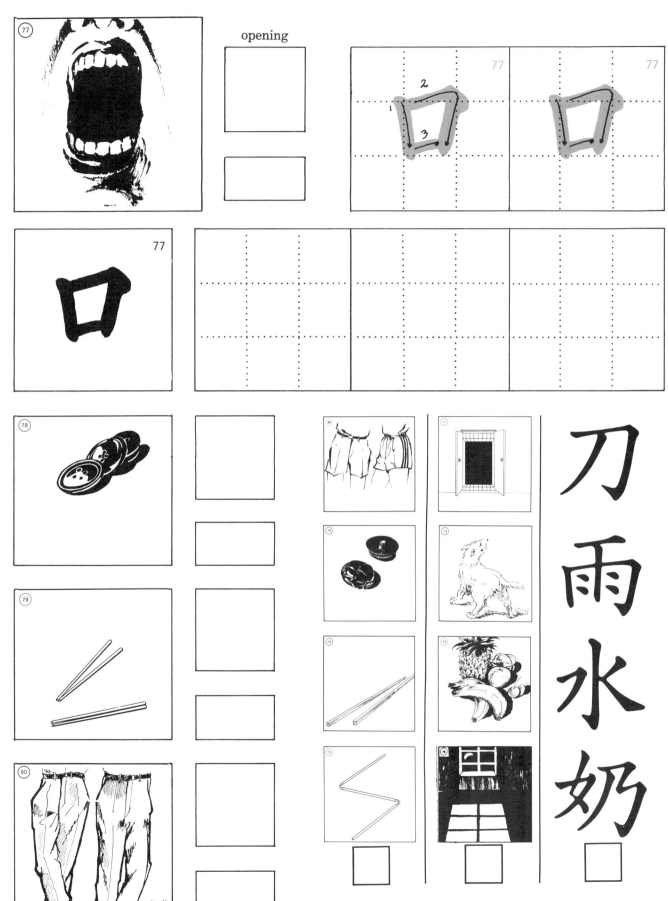

opening

Check the column that has common tones.

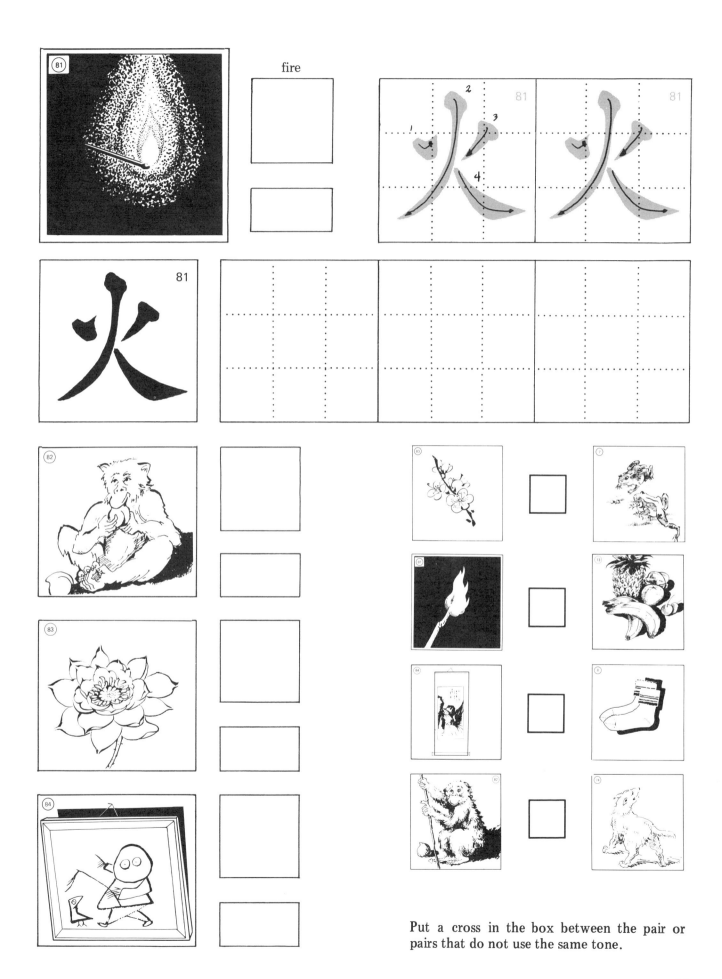

fire

Put a cross in the box between the pair or pairs that do not use the same tone.

67

NOUNS WITH AN ENDING 子

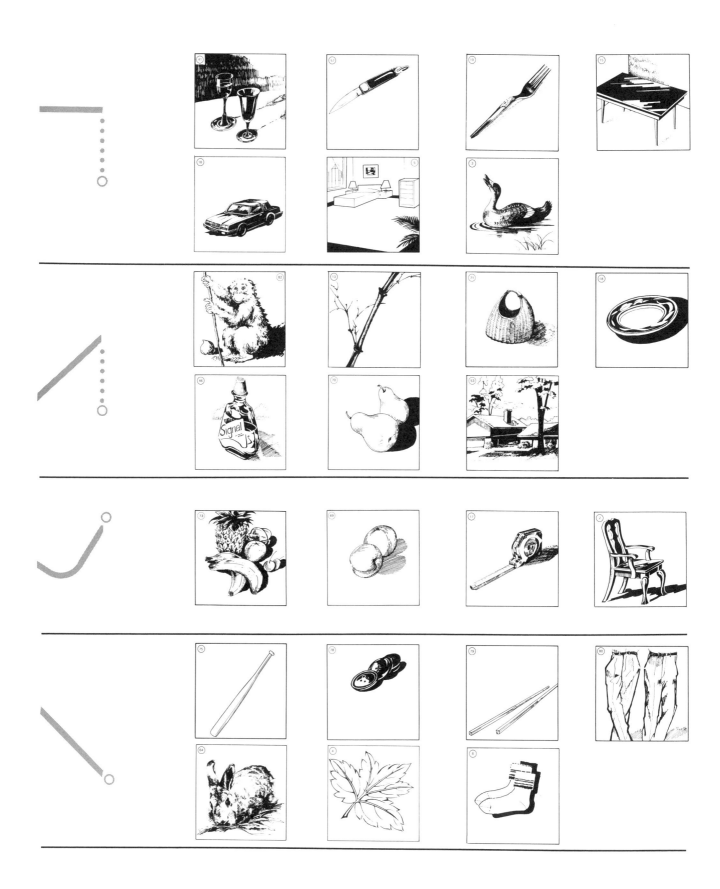

Flashcards

花 (83)	光 (76)	猴 (82)
狗 (74)	果 (73)	棍 (75)
火 (81)	口 (77)	褲 (80)
畫 (84)	釦 (78)	筷 (79)

果
狗
棍
光
口
釦
筷
褲
火
猴
花
畫

Flashcards

果		
狗		
棍		
光		
口		
扣		
筷		
裤		
火		
猴		
花		
画		

猴 82	光 76	花 83
棍 75	果 73	狗 74
裤 80	口 77	火 81
筷 79	扣 78	画 84

Initial Sounds

  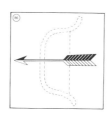  

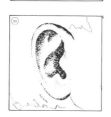

ORAL DRILL   (JǏ)

1. What's the number?   ZHÈ SHÌ JǏ?

2. What day is today?   JĪN TIĀN JǏ HÀO? XĪNG QĪ JǏ?

3. Is this the number _____ or not ?   ZHÈ SHÌ _____ BÚ SHÌ ?

4. Where are you? Here, there.   NǏ ZÀI NAR? ZHÈR NÀR.

5. How about here?   ZHÈR ZĚNME YÀNG?

6. Do you like it?   NǏ XǏHUAN MA?

7. The numbers 2, 7 and 9 ·   ÈR, QĪ, JIǓ

8. The color green   QĪNG (e.g. QĪNGWĀ   frog)
                                                          (QĪNGCÀI   green vegetables)

Pronunciation Guide

Phonetic Symbols		Pronunciation Key
PINYIN	**BOPOMOFO**	
J	ㄐ ㄐ	say "**jee**" as in ***jee**p*
Q	ㄑ ㄑ	say "**chee**" as in ***chee**se*
X	ㄒ ㄒ	say "**shee**" as in ***shee**p*
IANG	ㄧㄤ	say "**young**"
IONG	ㄩㄥ	say "**ee**" and "**ong**" together quickly
IN	ㄧㄣ	say "**in**"
ÜAN	ㄩㄢ	say "**you**" and "**an**" together quickly
ÜN	ㄩㄣ	say "**you**" and "**in**" together quickly
ER	ㄦ	say "**er**" as in **h*er***

Flashcards

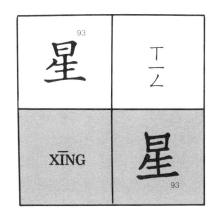

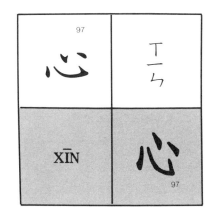

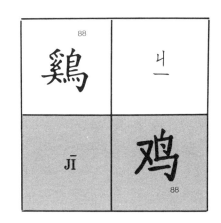

Flashcards

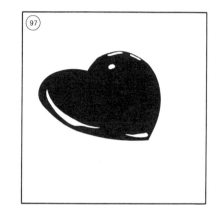

85

86

98

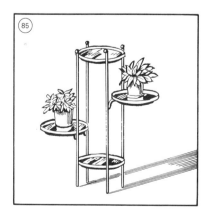

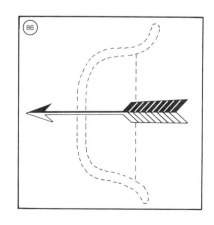

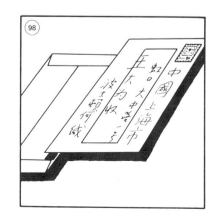

Flashcards

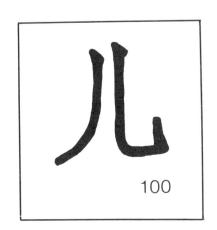

100

Flashcards

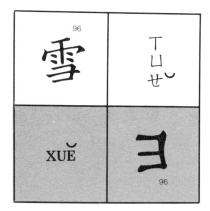

雪 ⁹⁶	ㄒㄩㄝˋ
XUĚ	ㅋ ⁹⁶

球 ⁸⁹	ㄑㄧㄡˊ
QIÚ	球 ⁸⁹

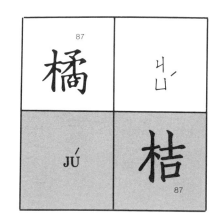

橘 ⁸⁷	ㄐㄩ
JÚ	桔 ⁸⁷

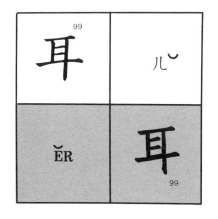

耳 ⁹⁹	ㄦˇ
ĚR	耳 ⁹⁹

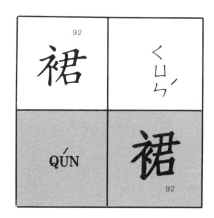

裙 ⁹²	ㄑㄩㄣˊ
QÚN	裙 ⁹²

牆 ⁹⁰	ㄑㄧㄤˊ
QIÁNG	墙 ⁹⁰

鞋 ⁹⁵	ㄒㄧㄝˊ
XIÉ	鞋 ⁹⁵

熊 ⁹⁴	ㄒㄩㄥˊ
XIÓNG	熊 ⁹⁴

兒 **100**

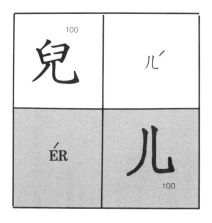

兒 ¹⁰⁰	ㄦˊ
ÉR	儿 ¹⁰⁰

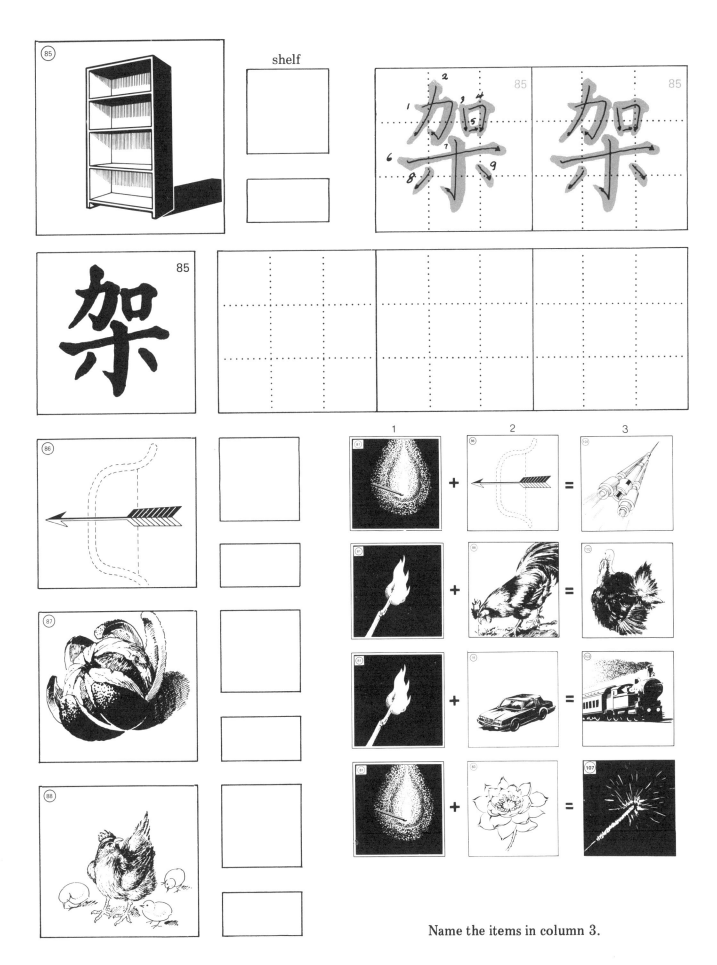

shelf

Name the items in column 3.

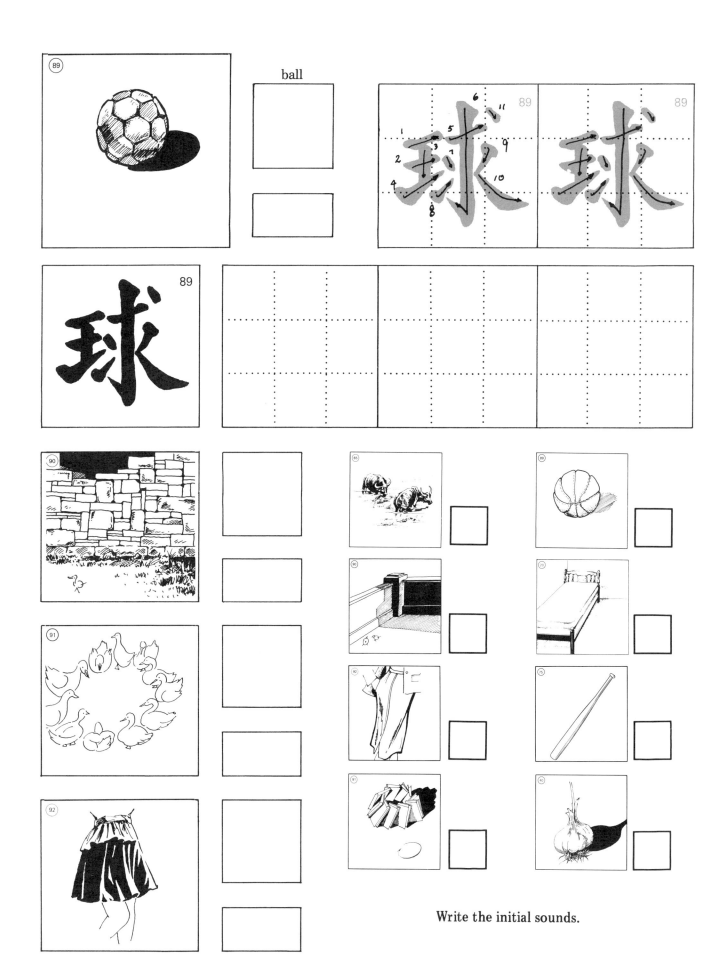

ball

Write the initial sounds.

78

star

Name the items in column 3.

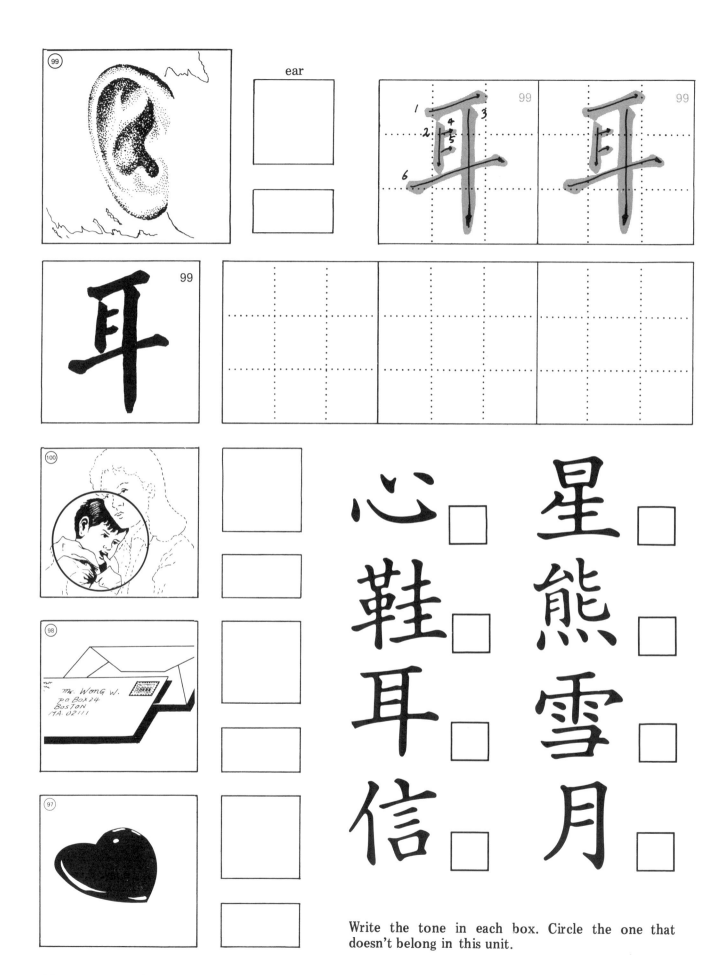

ear

Write the tone in each box. Circle the one that doesn't belong in this unit.

Flashcards

87 橘	89 球	90 牆
92 裙	94 熊	95 鞋
88 鶏	91 圈	96 雪
93 星	97 心	99 耳

兒	耳	信	心

架
箭
橘
鶏
球
牆
圈
裙
星
熊
鞋
雪

Flashcards

架	墙	球	桔
箭	90	89	87
桔	鞋	熊	裙
鸡	95	94	92
球			
墙	ⲋ	圈	鸡
圈	96	91	88
裙			
星	耳	心	星
熊	99	97	93
鞋			

ⲋ	心	信	耳	儿

EVALUATION 3

球 屋 牛 刀 衣 球 果 田

足 房 水 刺 雨 星 水 水

Beside each picture write the two characters that mean: raincoat, house, soccer ball, water buffalo, and planet.

NOUNS WITH AN ENDING 子

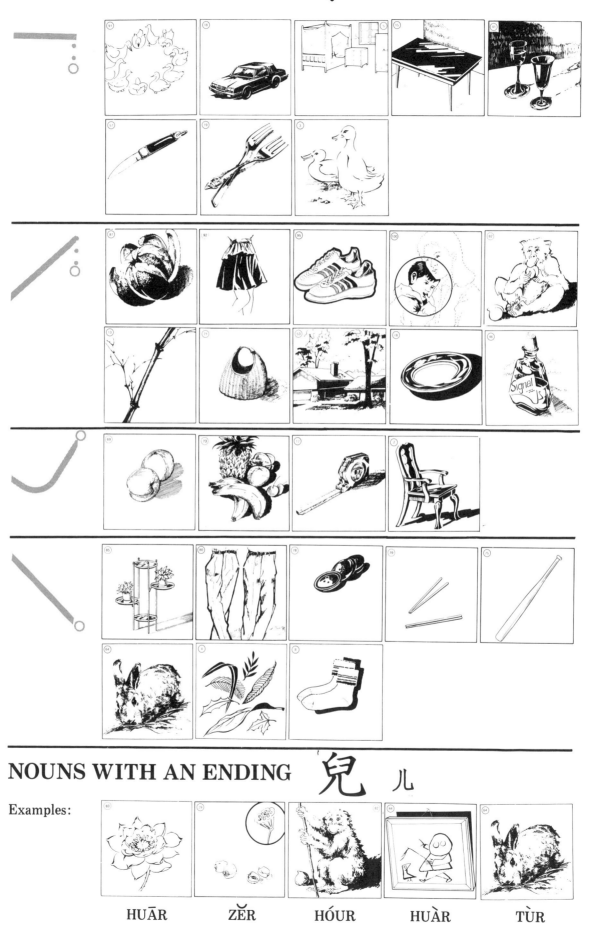

NOUNS WITH AN ENDING 兒 儿

Examples:

HUĀR   ZĚR   HÓUR   HUÀR   TÙR

What?
甚麼?(什么)

UNIT 8

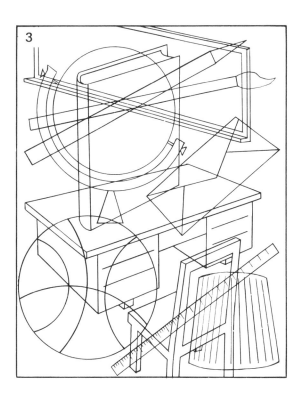

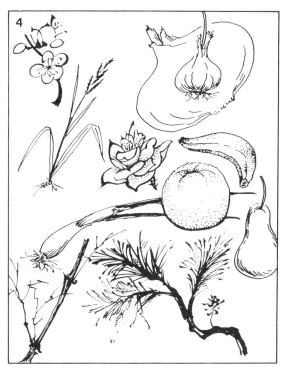

ORAL DRILL

What's this? Is this _____? Is this (a) _____ or not (a)_____? Is this _____ or _____?

85

椅	椅	屋	屋	桌	桌	紙	纸
書	书	人	人	字	字	傘	伞
報	报	筆	笔	瓶	瓶	墨	墨
棍	棍	畫	画	箭	架	架	箭
牆	墙	尺	尺	杯	杯	房	房
球	球						

葉	襪	玉	玉	桌	桌	牀	床
牌	牌	盤	盘	髮	发	燈	灯
果	果	鈕	扣	筷	筷	褲	裤
畫	画	箭	架	裙	裙	鞋	鞋
衣	衣	書	书	籃	篮	花	花
信	信						

水	水	樹	树	蕊	蕊	子	子
菜	菜	草	草	葱	葱	松	松
蒜	蒜	杯	杯	風	风	田	田
李	李	梨	梨	果	果	光	光
橘	桔	星	星	雪	彐	月	月
葉	叶	蛙	蛙	雨	雨	玉	玉
刺	刺	絲	丝	天	天	火	火

肉	肉	足	足	嘴	咀	報	报
貓	猫	馬	马	鳳	凤	髮	发
頭	头	兔	兔	牛	牛	奶	奶
鳥	鸟	龍	龙	狗	狗	口	口
鷄	鸡	熊	熊	心	心	耳	耳
窩	窝	魚	鱼	豬	猪	鼠	鼠
日	日	人	人	毛	毛	蛋	蛋
泥	泥	猴	猴				

Flashcards

101 這	103 甚	105 那
106 不	104 麼	102 是
		107 嗎

New Characters

101	這	ZHÈ (ZHÈI)	ㄓㄜ (ㄓㄟ)	this
105	那	NÀ (NÈI)	ㄋㄚ (ㄋㄟ)	that
102	是	SHÌ	ㄕ	to be
106	不	BÚ, BÙ	ㄅㄨ´; ㄅㄨ`	not, no
103	甚	SHÉN	ㄕㄣ ⎫	what (甚,麼)
104	麼	ME	.ㄇㄜ ⎭	
107	嗎	MA	.ㄇㄚ	a question mark

Flashcards

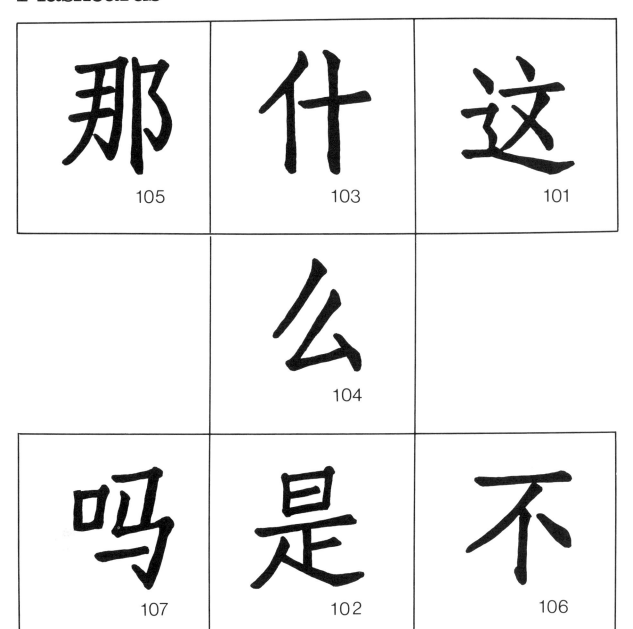

那 105	什 103	这 101
	么 104	
吗 107	是 102	不 106

New Characters

101	这	ZHÈ (ZHÈI)	ㄓㄜ (ㄓㄟ)	this
105	那	NÀ (NÈI)	ㄋㄚ (ㄋㄟ)	that
102	是	SHÌ	ㄕ	to be
106	不	BÚ, BÙ	ㄅㄨˊ; ㄅㄨ	not, no
103	什	SHÉN	ㄕㄣ	} what (什么)
104	么	ME	.ㄇㄜ	
107	吗	MA	.ㄇㄚ	a question mark

88

Trace and Write

Trace and Write

这 这 这

是 是 是

什 什 什

么 么 么

那 那 那

不 不 不

吗 吗 吗

90

Sentence Patterns

1. 這是甚麼？
   This   is   what

   What is this?

   這是書。
   This   is   book.

   This is a book .

---

2. 那 是 甚 麼 ？
   That   is   what

   What is that?

   那 是 筆。
   That   is   pen.

   That is a pen .

---

3. 這是紙嗎？
   This   is   paper   ?

   Is this paper ?

   是。
   Is.

   Yes.

---

4. 那是墨嗎？
   That   is   inkstick   ?

   Is that an inkstick ?

   不是。
   Not   is.

   No.

* Substitute the nouns found on pages 93 and 94.

Sentence Patterns

1. **What is this?**

   This is a book .

   这 是 什 么?
   This   is   what

   这 是 书*。
   This   is   book.

---

2. **What is that?**

   That is a pen .

   那 是 什 么?
   That   is   what

   那 是 笔*。
   That   is   pen.

---

3. **Is this paper ?**

   Yes.

   这 是 纸* 吗?
   This   is   paper   ?

   是。
   Is.

---

4. **Is that an inkstick ?**

   No.

   那 是 墨* 吗?
   That   is   inkstick   ?

   不 是。
   Not   is.

* Substitute the nouns found on pages 93 and 94.

92

1st Tone

What's this?

2nd Tone

What's that?

3rd Tone

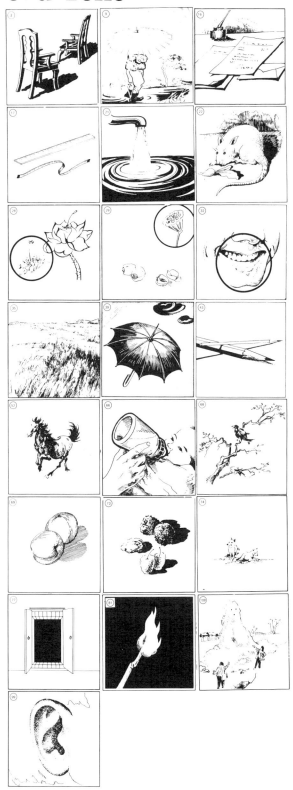

Is this _____?

94

4th Tone

Is that _____?

EVALUATION 4

Reading and Speaking

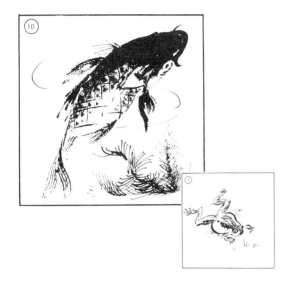

這 是 甚 麼?
這 是 魚。
甚 麼 不 是 魚?

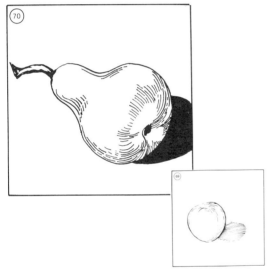

那 是 梨 嗎?
是。
甚 麼 不 是 梨?

這 是 龍 嗎?
是。
甚 麼 不 是 龍?

DRAW YOUR OWN

Fill in the 3 boxes with a Chinese character or phonetic transcription.

95

这 是 什 么?

这 是 鱼。

什 么 不 是 鱼?

那 是 梨 吗?

是。

什 么 不 是 梨?

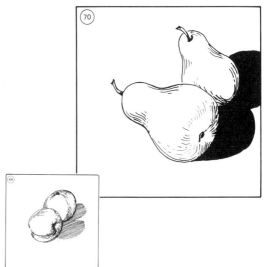

这 是 龙 吗?

是。

什 么 不 是 龙?

DRAW YOUR OWN

Fill in the three boxes with a Chinese character or phonetic transcription.

Who?

I'm the teacher, and you?   I'm _____.

您

you (polite)

我 是老师,你呢?   我 是 _____。

Are you _____?   Yes, I'm _____.

我

I, me

您是马老师吗? 是 的, 我 是马老师。

ORAL DRILL

Who are you?

Are you _____ ?

Are you _____ or not _____?

Are you _____ or _____ ?

What is this?

Is this _____?

Is this _____ or not _____?

Is this _____ or _____?

he, him

Is he the teacher? No, he isn't.

他是老师吗? 不,他不是老师。

Who's she? She is the teacher.

she, her

她是谁? 她是李老师。

Introductions

我 是＿＿＿＿＿＿＿＿＿。
(his name)

您 呢?

我 是＿＿＿＿＿＿＿＿＿。
(her name)

您 呢?

我 是＿＿＿＿＿＿＿＿＿。
(teacher's name)

您 呢?

SELF PORTRAIT

Questions and Answers

她 是 _____?
_{who}
Who is she?

她 是 _____。 She is ___ .

是 _____?
_{who}
Who is it?

是 _____。 It's me.
_{me}

那 是 _____?
_{what}
What's that?

那 是 _____。 It's a panda.

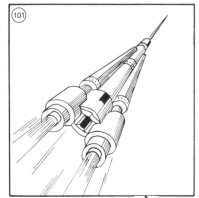

這 是 _____?
_{what}
What's this?

這 是 _____。 It's a rocket.

Note: 它 is used for inanimate objects and 牠 is used for animate objects. "It" is often used as a subject in English sentences, but when translated into Chinese, "it" is omitted. Begin the sentence with the verb or use "this" or "that" as the subject.

New Characters (traditional)

108	我	ㄨㄛˇ	I, me
109	你	ㄋㄧˇ	you
110	您	ㄋㄧㄣˊ	you (polite form)
111	呢	ㄋㄜ	sentence particle (has no meaning by itself)
112	大	ㄉㄚˋ	big, large
113	小	ㄒㄧㄠˇ	small, little, young (age)
114	老	ㄌㄠˇ	old 老鼠 mouse
115	師	ㄕ	teacher, master 老師
116	他	ㄊㄚ	he, him
117	她	ㄊㄚ	she, her
118	誰	ㄕㄟˊ ㄕㄨㄟˊ	who, whom
119	它	ㄊㄚ	it (things)

Note: For phonetic transcriptions in the Pinyin system, see page 102.

New Characters (simplified)

108	我	WǑ	I, me
109	你	NǏ	you
110	您	NÍN	you (polite form)
111	呢	NE	sentence particle (has no meaning by itself)
112	大	DÀ	big, large
113	小	XIǍO	small, little, young (age)
114	老	LǍO	old 老鼠 mouse
115	师	SHĪ	teacher, master 老师
116	他	TĀ	he, him
117	她	TĀ	she, her
118	谁	SHUÍ, SHÉI	who, whom
119	它	TĀ	it (things)

Note: For phonetic transcriptions in the BoPoMoFo system, see page **101**.

Flashcards

108 我

109 你

116 他

118 誰

110 您

117 她

114 老

111 呢

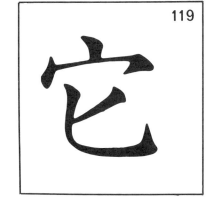

119 它

115 師

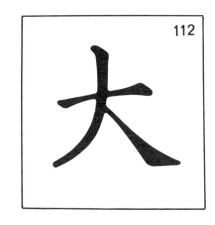

112 大

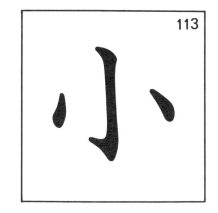

113 小

Flashcards

116

109

108

117

110

118

119

111

114

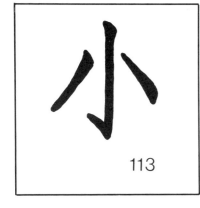

113

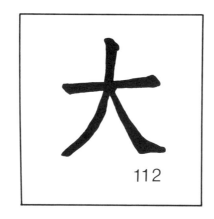

112

115

Trace and Write

我	我		你	
你				
您	您		呢	
呢				
大	大		小	
小				
老	老		師	
師				
他	他		她	
她				
誰	誰		它	
它				

Trace and Write

我	我		你	
你				
您	您		呢	
呢				
大	大		小	
小				
老	老		师	
师				
他	他		她	
她				
谁	谁		它	
它				

EVALUATION 5 (Pronunciation)

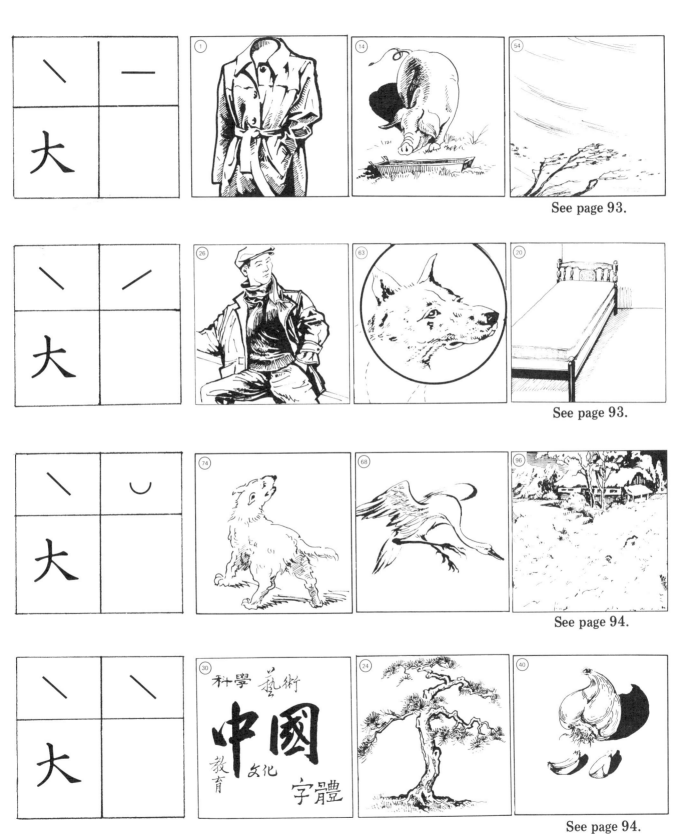

See page 93.

See page 93.

See page 94.

See page 94.

Use "big, large" to identify the 12 pictures using the following sentence pattern:

ZHÈ SHÌ_____BÚ SHÌ_____。

The Change of Tones

See page 93.

See page 93.

See page 94.

See page 94.

Use "small, little" to identify the 12 pictures using the following sentence pattern:

NÀ SHÌ _____ BÚ SHÌ _____ 。

Write the character for "big" or "small" in the 8 blank squares.

109

Reading

她是老＿＿，
teacher

不是老鼠。

那是老鼠，

不是小兔子。

那是小兔子，

不是大＿＿。

那是大＿＿，

不是＿＿＿＿＿。
STUDENT'S ANSWER

110

Whose?

誰 的   谁 的

ORAL DRILL

Whose is this? Is this _____'s? Is this _____'s or not _____'s? Is this _____'s or _____'s?

李書雨　田心竹　李玉鳳　李天龍　李美鳳

New Characters (traditional)

120	學	ㄒㄩㄝˊ	to learn	學 生	student
121	生	ㄕㄥ	new, raw, birth		
122	爸	ㄅㄚˋ	father	爸 爸	
123	媽	ㄇㄚ	mother	媽 媽	
124	也	ㄧㄝˇ	also		
125	和	ㄏㄜˊ	and		
126	的	˙ㄉㄜ	indicating possession or modification		
127	男	ㄋㄢˊ	male	男 孩	boy
128	孩	ㄏㄞˊ	child, kid	孩 子	child or children
129	女	ㄋㄩˇ	female	女 孩	girl
130	們	˙ㄇㄣ	indicating more than one person		
131	都	ㄉㄡ	both, all		

New Characters (simplified)

120	学	XUÉ	to learn	学 生	student
121	生	SHĒNG	new, raw, birth		
122	爸	BÀ	father	爸 爸	
123	妈	MĀ	mother	妈 妈	
124	也	YĚ	also		
125	和	HÉ	and		
126	的	DE	indicating possession or modification		
127	男	NÁN	male	男 孩	boy
128	孩	HÁI	child, kid	孩 子	child or children
129	女	NŬ	female	女 孩	girl
130	们	MEN	indicating more than one person		
131	都	DŌU	both, all		

Flashcards

120 學	121 生	122 爸
125 和	124 也	123 媽
131 都	127 男	126 的
130 們	129 女	128 孩

Flashcards

122

121

120

123

124

125

126

127

131

128

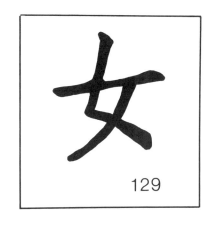

129

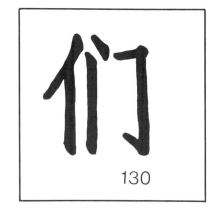

130

Trace and Write

學生爸媽也和的男孩女們都	學		生	
	爸		媽	
	也		和	
	的		男	
	孩		女	
	們		都	

Trace and Write

学生	学		生	
爸妈	爸		妈	
也和	也		和	
的男	的		男	
孩女	孩		女	
们都	们		都	

Read Aloud

也　also

她是老師，
他也是。

我是學生，
你也是。

這是杯子，
那也是。

DRAW

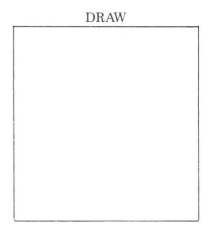

那是球，
這也是。

119

Read Aloud

也 also

她是老师，
他也是。

我是学生，
你也是。

这是杯子，
那也是。

DRAW

那是球，
这也是。

Oral Drill

和 and

ZHÈ SHÌ_____ HÉ_____。

NÀ SHÌ_____ HÉ_____。

Oral Drill 的 (possessive form)

This is _____'s _____. ZHÈ SHÌ _____ DE _____ 。

Read Aloud

們 (plural form for people)

老師們

他們是老師。

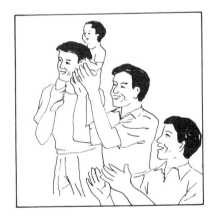

學生們

我們是學生。

爸爸們

他們是爸爸。

媽媽們

她們是媽媽。

Read Aloud

们 (plural form for people)

老师们

他们是老师。

学生们

我们是学生。

爸爸们

他们是爸爸。

妈妈们

她们是妈妈。

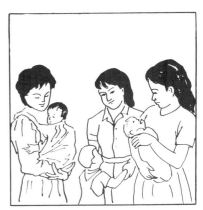

EVALUATION 6

Read aloud

也 和 都 們 的

我是學生,
你也是學生,
我和你都是學生。

鞋子是我的,
襪子也是我的,
鞋子和襪子都是我的。

DRAW

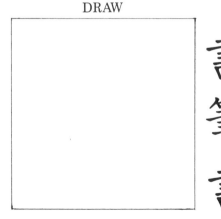

書是他們的,
筆也是他們的,
書和筆都是他們的。

EVALUATION 6

Read aloud 也 和 都 们 的

我 是 学 生,
你 也 是 学 生,
我 和 你 都 是 学 生。

鞋 子 是 我 的,
袜 子 也 是 我 的,
鞋 子 和 袜 子 都 是 我 的。

DRAW

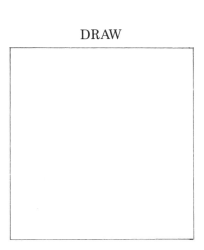

书 是 他 们 的,
笔 也 是 他 们 的,
书 和 笔 都 是 他 们 的。

126

UNIT 11

幾個 (几个)　幾隻 (几只)

HOW MANY?　WHAT NUMBER?

WHICH ONE?

| 1 | I | 一 | 6 | VI | 六 |

WHICH DOG?

| 2 | II | 二 | 7 | VII | 七 |

HOW MANY CATS DO YOU HAVE?

| 3 | III | 三 | 8 | VIII | 八 |

| 4 | IV | 四 | 9 | IX | 九 |

HOW MANY PIECES OF ____?

| 5 | V | 五 | 10 | X | 十 |

HOW MANY DO YOU HAVE?　　HOW OLD ARE YOU?

哪個 (哪个)　哪隻 (哪只)

127

Count and Sing*

SHÍ ZHĪ XIǍO BÁI MĀO

ㄕ ㄓ ㄒㄧㄠˇ ㄅㄞˊ ㄇㄠ

*to the tune of "Ten Little Indians"

New Characters (traditional)

No.	Character	Pronunciation	Meaning
132	一	ㄧ	one
133	二	ㄦˋ	two
134	三	ㄙㄢ	three
135	四	ㄙˋ	four
136	五	ㄨˇ	five
137	六	ㄌㄡˋ	six
138	七	ㄑㄧ	seven
139	八	ㄅㄚ	eight
140	九	ㄐㄧㄡˇ	nine
141	十	ㄕˊ	ten
142	幾	ㄐㄧˇ	How many?
143	個	˙ㄍㄜ	measure word for unit of
144	兩	ㄌㄧㄤˇ	two (pieces of)
145	隻	ㄓ	part of (an animal)
146	歲	ㄙㄨㄟˋ	age
147	叫	ㄐㄧㄠˋ	to call, to be called
148	名	ㄇㄧㄥˊ	name
149	那	ㄋㄚˋ, ㄋㄟˋ	which
150	國	ㄍㄨㄛˊ	country (nation)
151	中	ㄓㄨㄥ	middle; China
152	美	ㄇㄟˇ	beautiful; USA
153	沒	ㄇㄟˊ	don't have, didn't have
154	有	ㄧㄡˇ	to have
155	白	ㄅㄞˊ	white

New Characters (simplified)

No.	Character	Pinyin	Meaning
132	一	YĪ	one
133	二	ÈR	two
134	三	SĀN	three
135	四	SÌ	four
136	五	WǓ	five
137	六	LIÙ	six
138	七	QĪ	seven
139	八	BĀ	eight
140	九	JIǓ	nine
141	十	SHÍ	ten
142	几	JǏ	How many?
143	个	GE	measure word for unit of
144	两	LIǍNG	two (of)
145	只	ZHĪ	measure word for counting animals, etc.
146	岁	SUÌ	age
147	叫	JIÀO	to call, to be called
148	名	MÍNG	name
149	哪	NǍ (NĚI)	which
150	国	GUÓ	country (nation)
151	中	ZHŌNG	middle; China
152	美	MĚI	beautiful; USA
153	没	MÉI	don't have, didn't have
154	有	YǑU	to have
155	白	BÁI	white

Flashcards

132 一	133 二	134 三
135 四	136 五	137 六
138 七	139 八	140 九
141 十	142 幾	143 個

Flashcards

三

134

二

133

一

132

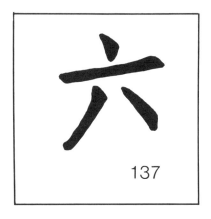

六

137

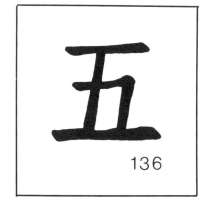

五

136

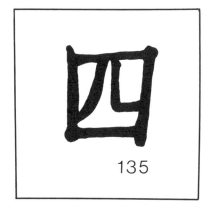

四

135

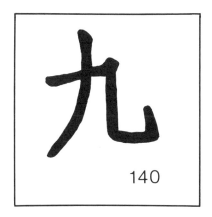

九

140

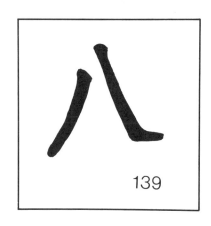

八

139

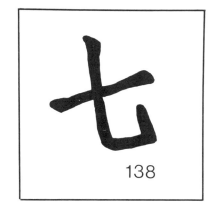

七

138

个

143

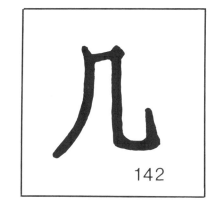

几

142

十

141

Flashcards

144 兩

145 隻

146 歲

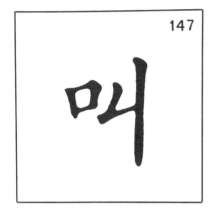

147 叫

148 名

149 哪

150 國

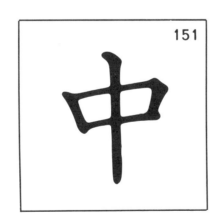

151 中

152 美

153 沒

154 有

155 白

Flashcards

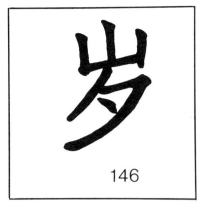

146

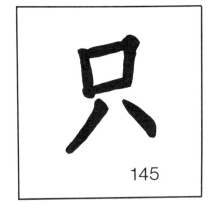

145

144

149

148

147

152

151

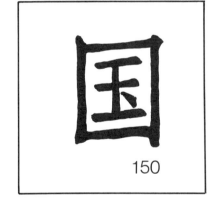

150

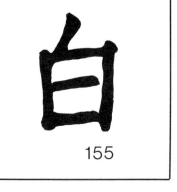

155

154

153

Read Aloud

一　二　三　，　三　二　一

一　二　三　四　五　六　七

七　六　五　四　三　二　一

三　二　三　四　五　六　七

七　五　六　四　二　三　一

一　一　二　二　三　三　四

四　四　三　三　二　二　一

四　五　六　，　六　五　七

七　八　九　，　九　八　七

七　八　九　九　八　十　一

Read across and read vertically, too.

135

Trace and Write

1	一	一	一			
2	二	二	二			
3	三	三	三			
4	四	四	四			
5	五	五	五			
6	六	六	六			
7	七	七	七			
8	八	八	八			
9	九	九	九			
10	十	十	十			

Trace and Write

幾 幾 幾

個 個 個

兩 兩 兩

隻 隻 隻

歲 歲 歲

叫 叫 叫

名 名 名

Trace and Write

几
个
两
只
岁
叫
名

Trace and Write

哪　哪　哪

國　國　國

中　中　中

美　美　美

沒　沒　沒

有　有　有

白　白　白

Trace and Write

哪　哪　哪

国　国　国

中　中　中

美　美　美

没　没　没

有　有　有

白　白　白

140

Oral Drill

How many? 幾個? 几个? 幾隻? 几只?

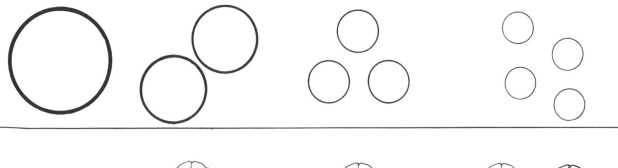

Note: Besides "GE" and "ZHĪ", there are many other measure words for counting, e.g.,
BĚN for books, ZHĀNG for tables, papers, beds, etc.

Oral Drill

What's the number? 這是幾? 这是几?

一　三　七　八

十
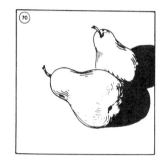

五　九

十
九

二　四　六

How many? 幾個? 几个? 幾隻? 几只?

142

to have 有 有　　to have not 沒有 没有

Write the character "to have" or "to have not" in the box to the right of each picture.

143

Read Aloud

也 和 都

他有大牛，
也有小牛。
他有大牛和小牛。
大牛和小牛他都有。

小狗是她的，
大狗也是她的。
小狗和大狗
都是她的。

Sentences

你 叫 甚 麼 名 字? What's your name?
You call what name ?

我 叫 _____。 My name is _____.
I call

你 幾 歲? How old are you?
You how many years old ?

我 _____ 歲。 I'm _____ years old.
I years old.

你 是 哪 國 人? What's your nationality?
You are which country person ?

我 是 美 國 人。 I am American.
I am American

你 有 狗 嗎? Do you have a dog?
You have dog ?

有/沒 有。 Yes/No.
Have / not have.

你 有 幾 隻 狗? How many dogs do you have?
You have how many dogs ?

我 有 兩 隻 狗。 I have two dogs.
I have two dogs.

145

Sentences

你叫什么名字？
You call what name ?

What's your name?

我叫 _____。
I call

My name is _____.

你 几 岁？
You how many years old ?

How old are you?

我 ____ 岁。
I years old.

I'm _____ years old.

你 是 哪 国 人？
You are which country person ?

What's your nationality?

我 是 美 国 人。
I am American .

I am American.

你 有 狗 吗？
You have dog ?

Do you have a dog?

有/没 有。
Have / not have .

Yes/No.

你 有 几 只 狗？
You have how many dogs ?

How many dogs do you have?

我 有 两 只 狗。
I have two dogs .

I have two dogs.

EVALUATION 7

Write your own dialogues in Chinese characters or phonetic transcriptions.

Are you Chinese? _____

No. _____

What's your nationality? _____

I'm American. _____

Write your own dialogues.

_____

_____

_____

_____

Note: 什麼 are the same as 甚麼, 什么.

CONVERSATION

UNIT 12

會話  会话

GOOD MORNING. I AM HERE.

DO YOU KNOW HOW TO SPEAK?

GOOD-BYE!

YOU DRAW WELL.

HOW ARE YOU?

ONE OR TWO?

TO WRITE. TO READ CHINESE. LISTEN. ONCE MORE. VERY GOOD!

LISTENING

ㄊㄧㄥ 聽

听 TĪNG

SPEAKING

ㄕㄨㄛ 説

SHUŌ 说

看
see

WRITING

ㄒㄧㄝ 寫 写 XIĚ

READING

ㄋㄧㄢˋ 念

念 NIÀN

WHICH ONE? OK! GIVE ME A PEN. DO YOU UNDERSTAND?

149

REVIEW

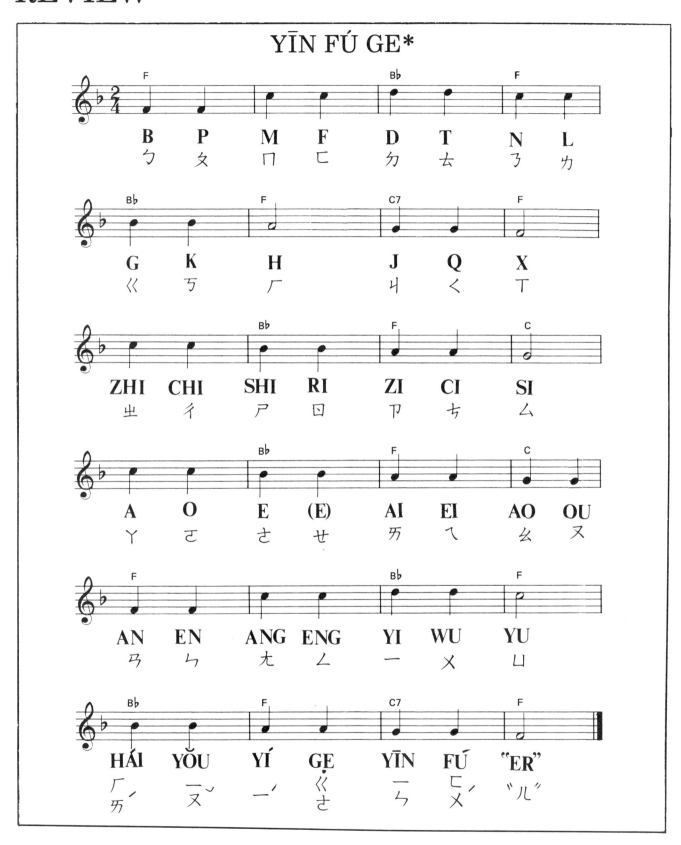

YĪN FÚ GE*

B P M F D T N L
P M F ㄅ ㄆ ㄇ ㄈ ㄉ ㄊ ㄋ ㄌ

G K H J Q X
ㄍ ㄎ ㄏ ㄐ ㄑ ㄒ

ZHI CHI SHI RI ZI CI SI
ㄓ ㄔ ㄕ ㄖ ㄗ ㄘ ㄙ

A O E (E) AI EI AO OU
ㄚ ㄛ ㄜ ㄝ ㄞ ㄟ ㄠ ㄡ

AN EN ANG ENG YI WU YU
ㄢ ㄣ ㄤ ㄥ ㄧ ㄨ ㄩ

HÁI YǑU YÍ GE YĪN FÚ "ER"
ㄏㄞˊ ㄧㄡˇ ㄧˊ ㄍㄜ ㄧㄣ ㄈㄨˊ "ㄦ"

*Known as the Chinese Alphabet Song and sung to the tune of the ABC Song.

一二三，一起唱! 再一次

Flashcards

156
會

157
念

158
寫

159
說

160
話

161
看

162
聽

163
跟

164
再

165
次

166
怎

167
得

Flashcards

158

157

156

161

160

159

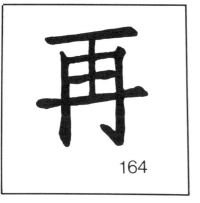

164

163

162

167

166

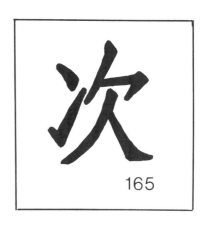

165

Flashcards

168 懂	169 點	170 給
171 唱	172 很	173 好
174 謝	175 起	176 見
177 還	178 要	179 在

Flashcards

170

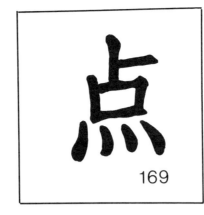

169

168

173

172

171

176

175

174

179

178

177

New Characters (traditional)

No.	Character	Phonetic	Meaning
156	會	ㄏㄨㄟˋ	can, know how to
157	念	ㄋㄧㄢˋ	to read aloud
158	寫	ㄒㄧㄝˇ	to write
159	說	ㄕㄨㄛ	to speak
160	話	ㄏㄨㄚˋ	language, spoken words
161	看	ㄎㄢˋ	to see, to look at
162	聽	ㄊㄧㄥ	to hear, to listen to
163	跟	ㄍㄣ	to follow, with, together with
164	再	ㄗㄞˋ	again
165	次	ㄘˋ	measure word for number of times
166	怎	ㄗㄣˇ	how
167	得	ㄉㄜ	used after a verb indicating "to be able to"
168	懂	ㄉㄨㄥˇ	to understand
169	點	ㄉㄧㄢˇ	dot, spot, point, a tiny bit
170	給	ㄍㄟˇ	to give
171	唱	ㄔㄤˋ	to sing
172	很	ㄏㄣˇ	very
173	好	ㄏㄠˇ	good, nice, fine
174	謝	ㄒㄧㄝˋ	to thank
175	起	ㄑㄧˇ	to get up, rise, 一起 together
176	見	ㄐㄧㄢˋ	to see, to meet
177	還	ㄏㄞˊ	still, in addition to
178	要	ㄧㄠˋ	to want
179	在	ㄗㄞˋ	to be in/at/on
180	了	ㄌㄜ	indicates completed action, changed status (a sentence part)
181	早	ㄗㄠˇ	early, good morning

Note: For phonetic transcriptions in the Pinyin system, see page 156.

New Characters (simplified)

No.	Character	Pinyin	Meaning
156	会	HUÌ	can, know how to
157	念	NIÀN	to read aloud
158	写	XIĚ	to write
159	说	SHUŌ	to speak
160	话	HUÀ	language, spoken words
161	看	KÀN	to see, to look at
162	听	TĪNG	to hear, to listen to
163	跟	GĒN	to follow, with, together with
164	再	ZÀI	again
165	次	CÌ	measure word for number of times
166	怎	ZĚN	how
167	得	DE	used after a verb indicating "to be able to"
168	懂	DŎNG	to understand
169	点	DIĂN	dot, spot, point, a tiny bit
170	给	GĚI	to give
171	唱	CHÀNG	to sing
172	很	HĚN	very
173	好	HǍO	good, nice, fine
174	谢	XIÈ	to thank
175	起	QǏ	to get up, rise; 一起 together
176	见	JIÀN	to see, to meet
177	还	HÁI	still, in addition to
178	要	YÀO	to want
179	在	ZÀI	to be in/at/on
180	了	LE	indicates completed action, changed status (a sentence part)
181	早	ZǍO	early, good morning

Note: For phonetic transcriptions in the BoPoMoFo system, see page 155.

Conversation 1

<table>
<tr><td colspan="2">

會 話 一

</td><td></td></tr>
</table>

會 話 一

一　你　會　嗎？
① You　can　？

會
Can

不　會
No　can

會　一　點　兒
Can　a　little　bit.

二　你　會　説　嗎
② You　can　speak　？

寫
write

念
read

畫
draw

三　你　會　説　中　國　話　嗎？
③ You　can　speak　China　language　？

寫　　　　字
write　　characters

念　　　　書
read　　books

畫　　　　畫 兒
draw　　pictures

四　聽　我　説。
④ Listen　me　speak.

念
read

唱
sing

五　跟　我　念。
⑤ Follow　me　read.

唱
Sing

1. Can you _____?

Yes.

No.

A little bit.

2. Can you [speak]?

   [write]

   [read]

   [draw]

3. Can you [speak] the Chinese *language?*

   Can you [write] Chinese *characters?*

   Can you [read] a Chinese book?

   Can you [draw] Chinese pictures?

4. Listen to me (while I) speak.

   read.

   sing.

5. Read after me.

   Sing.

157

会 话 一   Conamentversation 1

一 你 会 吗 ?
① You can ?

会
Can

不 会
No can

会 一 点 儿
Can a little bit

二 你 会 说 吗
② You can speak ?

写
write

念
read

画
draw

三 你 会 说 中 国 话 吗 ?
③ You can speak China language ?

写   字
write   characters

念   书
read   books

画   画 儿
draw   pictures

四 听 我 说 。
④ Listen me speak.

念
read

唱
sing

五 跟 我 念 。
⑤ Follow me read.

唱
sing

1. Can you _____?

   Yes.

   No.

   A little bit.

2. Can you [speak]?

   [write]

   [read]

   [draw]

3. Can you [speak] the Chinese *language?*

   Can you [write] Chinese *characters?*

   Can you [read] a Chinese book?

   Can you [draw] Chinese *pictures?*

4. Listen to me (while I) speak.

   read.

   sing.

5. Read after me.

   Sing after me.

158

會 話 二

一
① 你 好 嗎 ?
　　You fine ?

你的 老師 好 嗎 ?
Your teacher fine ?

爸 爸
father

媽 媽
mother

狗
dog

貓
cat

二
② 很 好, 謝 謝。
Very good, thank thank.

三
③ 給 我 一 個 蛋, 好 嗎 ?
Give me one ( ) egg, OK ?

一 隻 鷄
one ( ) chicken

兩 個 梨
two ( ) pear

四
④ 好 的。
OK.

五
⑤ 你 説 得 很 好。
You speak ( ) very good.

念
read

寫
write

畫
draw

六
⑥ 謝 謝。
Thank thank.

七
⑦ 不 謝。
Not thank.

1. How are you?

　How is your *teacher?*

　　　father

　　　mother

　　　dog

　　　cat

2. Fine, thanks (thank you).

3. Give me an *egg*, OK?

　　a *chicken*

　　two pears

4. O.K.

5. You *speak* well.

　　read

　　write

　　draw

6. Thanks.

7. No matter
(don't mention it).

159

Conversation 2

① 你 好 吗?
    You fine ?

你 的 老 师 好 吗?
Your teacher fine ?

爸 爸
father

妈 妈
mother

狗
dog

猫
cat

二 很 好, 谢 谢。
② Very good, thank thank.

三 给 我 一 个 蛋, 好 吗?
③ Give me one ( ) egg, OK ?

一 只 鸡
one ( ) chicken

两 个 梨
two ( ) pear

四 好 的。
④ OK.

五 你 说 得 很 好。
⑤ You speak ( ) very good.

念
read

写
write

画
draw

六 谢 谢。
⑥ Thank thank.

七 不 谢。
⑦ Not thank

1. How are you?

   How is your *teacher?*

     father

     mother

     dog

     cat

2. Fine, thanks (thank you).

3. Give me an *egg*, OK?

   a *chicken*

   two pears

4. O.K.

5. You *speak* well.

   read

   write

   draw

6. Thanks.

7. No matter
(don't mention it).

Conversation 3

一
① 你 要 甚 麼?
You want what ?
我 要 燈。

1. What do you want?

   I want [a lamp].

二
② 你 要 哪 個?
You want which one ?
我 要 這 個。

2. Which one do you want?

   I want [this one].

三
③ 你 要 幾 個?
You want how many ?
我 要 兩 個。

3. How many do you want?

   I want [two].

四
④ 你 要 牛 奶 嗎?
You want cow milk ?
不 要。

4. Do you want [milk]?

   No.

五
⑤ 你 要 橘 子 嗎?
You want orange ?
要。

5. Do you want [an orange]?

   Yes.

六
⑥ 還 要 甚 麼?
Still want what ?
還 要 梨 和 李 子。

6. Do you want [anything else]?

   I want more [pears and plums].

七
⑦ 還 要 甚 麼?
Still want what ?
不 要 了, 謝 謝。
No more want , thank thank.

7. Do you want [anything else]?

   No more, thanks.

八
⑧ 你 媽 媽 在 嗎?
Your mother in ?

8. Is your mother in?

九
⑨ 在。

9. Yes (in).

十
⑩ 不 在。

10. No (not in).

  * 要 不 要 can be replaced with 有 沒 有

会 话 三

一
①
你 要 什么?
You want what ?

我 要 灯。

二
②
你 要 哪 个?
You want which one ?

我 要 这 个。

三
③
你 要 几 个?
You want how many ?

我 要 两 个。

四
④
你 要 牛奶 吗?
You want cow milk ?

不 要。

五
⑤
你 要 桔子 吗?
You want orange ?

要。

六
⑥
还 要 什么?
Still want what ?

还 要 梨 和 李子。

七
⑦
还 要 什么?
Still want what ?

不 要 了 谢 谢。
No more want , thank thank.

八
⑧
你 妈 妈 在 吗?
Your mother in ?

九
⑨
在。

十
⑩
不 在。

Conversation 3

1. What do you want?

   I want a lamp .

2. Which one do you want?

   I want this one .

3. How many do you want?

   I want two .

4. Do you want milk ?

   No.

5. Do you want an orange ?

   Yes.

6. Do you want anything else ?

   I want more pears and plums .

7. Do you want anything else ?

   No more, thanks.

8. Is your mother in?

9. Yes (in).

10. No (not in).

*要 不 要 **can be replaced with** 有 没 有

162

會話四

Conversation 4

一 這個字怎麼念？
① This (one) word how read ?
那 寫
That write

1. How do you *read this* character?
write that

二 "No more" 中國話怎麼說？
② China language how say ?
中國話說"沒了"。
China language say "no more".

2. How do you say "no more" in Chinese?

In Chinese we say ㄇㄟˊㄌㄜ˙.

三 "小狗"美國話怎麼說？
③ "Small dog" U.S.A. language how say ?
美國話說 "puppy".
U.S.A. language say "puppy".

3. How do you say ㄒㄧˇㄠ ㄍㄍㄡˇ in English?

In English we say "puppy".

四 你聽得懂嗎？
④ You hear ( ) understand?
聽得懂
Hear ( ) understand

4. Do you understand?

Yes.

五 你聽得見嗎？
⑤ You hear ( ) see ?
聽得見
Hear ( ) see.

5. Can you hear?

Yes.

六 你看得懂嗎？
⑥ You see ( ) understand?
看不懂
See not understand

6. Can you see and understand?

No.

七 再一次
⑦ Again one (time)
個
(unit)

7. Once more (again).

One more (unit)

八 再說一次
⑧ Again say one ( )
念
read
寫
write

8. *Speak* again (once more).

Read

Write

九 再見
⑨ Again see

9. See you (again). Goodbye!

一 ① 这 个 字 怎么 念？
This (one) word how read ?
那   写
That   write

1. How do you *read this* character?
   write that

二 ② "No more" 中 国 话 怎么 说？
China language how say ?

中 国 话 说 没 了。
China language say "no more".

2. How do you say "no more" in Chinese?

   In Chinese we say ___MÉILE___ .

三 ③ 小 狗 美 国 话 怎么 说？
Small dog U.S.A. language how say ?

美 国 话 说 "puppy"。
U.S.A. language say "puppy".

3. How do you say ___XIǍO GǑU___ in English?

   In English we say "puppy".

四 ④ 你 听 得 懂 吗？
You hear ( ) understand?

听 得 懂
Hear ( ) understand

4. Do you [understand]?

   Yes.

五 ⑤ 你 听 得 见 吗？
You hear ( ) see ?

听 得 见
Hear ( ) see

5. Can you [hear]?

   Yes.

六 ⑥ 你 看 得 懂 吗？
You see ( ) understand ?

看 不 懂
See not understand

6. Can you [see] and [understand]?

   No.

七 ⑦ 再 一 次
Again one ( )

个
(unit)

7. Once more (again).

   One more (unit)

八 ⑧ 再 说 一 次
Again say one (time)

念
read

写
write

8. *Speak* again (once more).

   Read

   Write

九 ⑨ 再 见
Again see

9. See you (again). Goodbye!

GREETINGS

Good Morning
early morning: ZĂO
formal: ZĂO ĀN
general: SHÀNG WŬ HĂO

Good Afternoon
formal: WŬ ĀN
general: XIÀ WŬ HĂO

Good Evening
WĂN SHÀNG HĂO

Good Night
WĂN ĀN

Hello!
attention: WÈI   greeting (formal): NĬ(N) HĂO

Health
general (formal): NĬ(N) HĂO MA?   How are you?
specific: NĬ SHĒNTI HĂO MA?   How are you feeling?

Courtesy

Thank You   General: XIÈ XIE
Enthusiasm: DUŌ XIÈ
(Reply): BÚ KÈ QI   You're welcome.

Apology   General: DUÌ BU QĬ   I'm sorry.
(Reply): MÉI GUĀN XI   That's okay.
Formal: HĚN BÀO QIÀN   I'm sorry.
(Reply): MÉI GUĀN XI   That's okay.

Forgiveness   QĬNG YUÁN LIÀNG   Please forgive me.
(Reply): MÉI GUĀN XI   That's okay.

Politeness   May I come in? WŎ KĚ YI JÌN LÁI MA?
Please come in. QĬNG JÌN
May I trouble you to . . . LÁO JIÀ (MÁ FAN NÍN)
Please sit down. QĬNG ZUÒ
Have some tea. QĬNG HĒ CHÁ

USEFUL SENTENCES

Asking Directions

Where is _____? _____ ZÀI NĂR?

The bathroom   CÈ SUŎ   The bus stop   CHĒ ZHÀN

The post office   YÓU JÚ

Reply   It's here: ZÀI ZHÈR   It's upstairs: ZÀI LÓU SHÀNG

It's there: ZÀI NÀR   It's downstairs: ZÀI LÓU XIÀ

Asking Help

Please help me. QĬNG BĀNG WŎ.

Please lead me to . . . QĬNG DÀI WŎ QÙ . . .

Please point the way. QĬNG NÍN ZHĬ GĔI WŎ KÀN.

Please write it down. QĬNG NÍN XIĔ XIÀ LÁI.

Please find someone who speaks English.

QĬNG ZHĂO YÍ GÈ DŎNG YĪNG YŬ DE RÉN.

Admiration

How wonderful!   HĂO JÍ LE!

How beautiful!   MĔI JÍ LE!

(He) is good-looking: (TĀ) HĔN HĂO KÀN.

It's very good.   HĔN HĂO

A. Food	HĔN HĂO CHĪ	It's delicious.
B. Music	HĔN HĂO TĪNG	It's musical.
C. Fun	HĔN HĂO WÁNR	It's fun.
D. Drink	HĔN HĂO HĒ	It's tasteful.
E. Tool	HĔN HĂO YÒNG	It's easy to use.

Don't (BÚ YÀO)

Silence!   QĬNG ĀN JÌNG

Shut up!   BÌ ZUĬ

Don't talk: BÚ YÀO SHUŌ HUÀ

No smoking: QĬNG WÙ XĪ YĀN

Don't touch⎫
Don't move⎭ :BÚ YÀO DÒNG

Extra Vocabulary

Measure Words (for)

Books:	BĚN
Pens:	ZHĪ
Paper, Beds, Tables, etc.	ZHĀNG
Clothing:	JIÀN
Rooms:	JIĀN
Cars:	LIÀNG
Meat, Land, Rocks, etc.	KUÀI
Chairs, Umbrellas, etc.	BĂ
Pants, Skirt, etc.	TIÁO
Pair of (Shoes, Socks, etc.)	SHUĀNG

USE: *NUMBER + MEASURE WORD + NOUN*

EXAMPLE: One book: YÌ *BĚN* SHŪ

Two books: LIĂNG *BĚN* SHŪ

Three books: SĀN *BĚN* SHŪ

Colors (YÁN SÈ)

Black: HĒI	Brown: ZŌNG	Yellow: HUÁNG	Purple: ZĬ
Gray: HUĪ	Red: HÓNG	Blue: LÁN	Green: LǙ

USE: Number + Measure Word + Color + Noun

E.G., A white dog. YÌ ZHĪ *BÁI* GŎU.

Number + Measure Word + Color + SÈ + DE + Noun

E.G., A white dog. YÌ ZHĪ *BÁI SÈ* DE GŎU.

Number + Measure Word + *YÁN SÈ* + DE + Noun

E.G., A white dog. YÌ ZHĪ *BÁI YÁN SÈ* DE GŎU.

Family Members

Father: BÀ BA (formal): FÙ QĪN	Younger Brother: DÌ DI
Mother: MĀ MA (formal): MŬ QĪN	Younger Sister: MÈI MEI
Elder Brother: GĒ GE	Son: ÉR ZĬ
Elder Sister: JIĚ JIE	Daughter: NǙ ÉR

Location words and their uses

Where is _____ ?	_____ ZÀI NĂR?	
It's *here.*	_____ ZÀI *ZHÈR.*	
there	_____ ZÀI NÀR	
on the table	_____ ZÀI ZHUŌ ZI	SHÀNG BIĀNR
under	_____	XIÀ BIĀNR
inside	_____	LĬ BIĀNR
outside	_____	WÀI BIĀNR
in front of	_____	QIÁN BIĀNR
behind	_____	HÒU BIĀNR
next to	_____	PÁNG BIĀNR
left of	_____	ZUŎ BIĀNR
right of	_____	YÒU BIĀNR

Character Numbers and Meanings

1. clothes
2. chair
3. duck
4. leaf
5. room
6. nest
7. frog
8. socks
9. rain
10. fish
11. jade
12. moon
13. bamboo
14. pig
15. table
16. paper
17. ruler
18. vehicle
19. fork
20. bed
21. water
22. mouse (rat)
23. book
24. tree
25. sun
26. people
27. meat
28. pistil (flower)
29. seed
30. Chinese character
31. foot
32. mouth
33. thorn
34. vegetable
35. grass
36. onion
37. pine
38. silk
39. umbrella
40. garlic
41. cup
42. newspaper
43. pen
44. ice
45. skin
46. bottle
47. cards
48. plate
49. fur
50. cat

51. inkstick
52. horse
53. house
54. wind
55. Phoenix
56. hair
57. knife
58. egg
59. lamp
60. jelly (gelatin)
61. field
62. sky
63. head
64. rabbit
65. cow
66. milk
67. mud
68. bird
69. plum
70. pear
71. basket
72. dragon
73. fruit
74. dog
75. stick
76. ray or beam
77. opening
78. button
79. chopsticks
80. pants
81. fire
82. monkey
83. flower
84. painting
85. shelf
86. arrow
87. orange
88. chicken
89. ball
90. wall
91. circle
92. skirt
93. star
94. bear
95. shoes
96. snow
97. heart
98. letters
99. ear
100. son

101. this
102. to be
103. } what (bound form)
104. }
105. that
106. not, no
107. question mark
108. I, me
109. you
110. you (polite)
111. sentence particle
112. big, large
113. small, little young (age)
114. old
115. teacher, master
116. he, him
117. she, her
118. who, whom
119. it (inanimate)
120. to learn
121. new, raw, birth
122. father
123. mother
124. also
125. and
126. possession form
127. male
128. child, kid
129. female
130. more than one person
131. both, all
132. one
133. two
134. three
135. four
136. five
137. six
138. seven
139. eight
140. nine
141. ten
142. how many?
143. measure word
144. two (of)
145. measure word
146. age
147. to call
148. name
149. which
150. country (nation)

151. middle; China
152. beautiful
153. to have not
154. to have
155. white
156. can, know how to
157. to read aloud
158. to write
159. to speak
160. language, speech
161. to see, to look at
162. to hear, to listen to
163. to follow, with
164. again
165. number of times (measure word)
166. how
167. to be able to, to gain
168. to understand
169. dot, spot, point
170. to give
171. to sing
172. very
173. good, nice, fine
174. to thank
175. to get up or rise
176. to see, to meet
177. still, in addition to
178. to want
179. to be in/at/on
180. sentence particle to indicate action completed or status changed
181. early, good morning

Initial Sound Vocabulary (Traditional)

B	杯	報	筆	冰	不	爸	八	白		
P	皮	瓶	牌	盤						
M	毛	貓	墨	馬	麼	嗎	媽	們	名	美	沒
F	房	風	鳳	髮						
D	刀	蛋	燈	凍	大	的	都	得	懂	點
T	田	天	頭	兔	他	她	它	聽		
N	牛	奶	泥	鳥	那	你	您	呢	男	女	哪	念
L	李	梨	籃	龍	老	六	兩	了		
G	果	狗	棍	光	個	國	跟	給		
K	口	釦	筷	褲	看					
H	火	猴	花	畫	和	孩	會	話	很	好	還
J	箭	架	橘	雞	九	幾	叫	見		
Q	球	牆	圈	裙	七	起				
X	星	熊	鞋	雪	心	信	小	學	寫	謝
ZH	竹	豬	桌	紙	這	隻	中			
CH	尺	車	叉	牀	唱					
SH	水	鼠	書	樹	是	甚	師	誰	生	十	說
R	日	人	肉	蕊						
Z	子	字	足	嘴	再	怎	在	早		
C	刺	菜	草	蔥	次					
S	松	絲	傘	蒜	三	四	歲			
Y	衣	椅	鴨	葉	也	一	有	要		
W	屋	窩	蛙	襪	我	五				
YU	雨	魚	玉	月						
ER	耳	兒	二							

Initial Sound Vocabulary (Simplified)

B	杯	报	笔	冰	不	爸	八	白		
P	皮	瓶	牌	盘						
M	毛	猫	墨	马	么	吗	妈	们	名	美	没
F	房	风	凤	发						
D	刀	蛋	灯	冻	大	的	都	得	懂	点
T	田	天	头	兔	他	她	它	听		
N	牛	奶	泥	鸟	那	你	您	呢	男	女	哪	念
L	李	梨	篮	龙	老	六	两	了		
G	果	狗	棍	光	个	国	跟	给		
K	口	扣	筷	裤	看					
H	火	猴	花	画	和	孩	会	话	很	好	还
J	架	箭	桔	鸡	九	几	叫	见		
Q	球	墙	圈	裙	七	起				
X	星	熊	鞋	彐	心	信	小	学	写	谢
ZH	竹	猪	桌	纸	这	只	中			
CH	尺	车	叉	床	唱					
SH	水	鼠	书	树	是	什	师	谁	生	十	说
R	日	人	肉	蕊						
Z	子	字	足	咀	再	怎	在	早		
C	刺	菜	草	葱	次					
S	松	丝	伞	蒜	三	四	岁			
Y	衣	椅	鸭	叶	也	一	有	要		
W	屋	窝	蛙	袜	我	五				
YU	雨	鱼	玉	月		**ER**	耳	儿	二	

Reference Vocabulary

English meaning	Traditional	BoPoMoFo	Simplified	Pinyin
a little bit	一點兒，一點點	ㄧㄉㄧㄢㄦ ㄧㄉㄧㄢ˙ㄉㄧㄢ	一点儿，一点点	YÌDIǍNR; YÌDIǍNDIAN
again	再	ㄗㄞ	再	ZÀI
age	歲	ㄙㄨㄟ	岁	SUÌ
all; both	都	ㄉㄡ	都	DŌU
also; too	也	ㄧㄝˇ	也	YĚ
American	美國人	ㄇㄟˇ ㄍㄨㄛˊ ㄖㄣˊ	美国人	MĚIGUÓRÉN
and	和	ㄏㄜˊ	和	HÉ
arrow	箭	ㄐㄧㄢ	箭	JIÀN
ball	球	ㄑㄧㄡˊ	球	QIÚ
bamboo	竹，竹子	ㄓㄨˊ，ㄓㄨˊ˙ㄗ	竹，竹子	ZHÚ, zhúzi
basket	籃，籃子	ㄌㄢˊ，ㄌㄢˊ˙ㄗ	篮，篮子	LÁN, lánzi
basketball	籃球	ㄌㄢˊ ㄑㄧㄡˊ	篮球	LÁNQIÚ
bear	熊	ㄒㄩㄥˊ	熊	XIÓNG
beautiful	美	ㄇㄟˇ	美	MĚI
bed	牀	ㄔㄨㄤˊ	床	CHUÁNG
big (large)	大	ㄉㄚˋ	大	DÀ
bird	鳥	ㄋㄧㄠˇ	鸟	NIǍO, niǎor
book	書	ㄕㄨ	书	SHŪ
bookshelf	書架	ㄕㄨ ㄐㄧㄚˋ	书架	SHŪJIÀ
bottle	瓶，瓶子	ㄆㄧㄥˊ，ㄆㄧㄥˊ˙ㄗ	瓶，瓶子	PÍNG, píngzi

English meaning	Traditional	BoPoMoFo	Simplified	Pinyin
boy	男孩子	ㄋㄢˊ ㄏㄞˊ˙ㄗ	男孩子	NÁN HÁIZI
button	鈕，鈕子	ㄎㄡˋ, ㄎㄡˋ˙ㄗ	扣，扣子	KÒU, kòuzi
car	車，車子	ㄔㄜ, ㄔㄜ˙ㄗ	车，车子	CHĒ, chēzi
cards	牌	ㄆㄞˊ	牌	PÁI
cat	貓	ㄇㄠ	猫	MĀO
chair	椅，椅子	ㄧˇ, ㄧˇ˙ㄗ	椅，椅子	YĬ, yǐzi
characters (written words)	字	ㄗˋ	字	ZÌ
chicken	鷄	ㄐㄧ	鸡	JĪ
child (children)	子，孩子	ㄗˇ, ㄏㄞˊ˙ㄗ	子，孩子	ZĬ; háizi
China	中國	ㄓㄨㄥ ㄍㄨㄛˊ	中国	ZHŌNGGUÓ
Chinese	中國人	ㄓㄨㄥ ㄍㄨㄛˊ ㄖㄣˊ	中国人	ZHŌNGGUÓRÉN
chopsticks	筷，筷子	ㄎㄨㄞˋ, ㄎㄨㄞˋ˙ㄗ	筷，筷子	KUÀI, kuàizi
circle	圈	ㄑㄩㄢ	圈	QUĀN
clothes	衣	ㄧ	衣	YĪ
clothes hanger	衣架	ㄧ ㄐㄧㄚˋ	衣架	YĪ JIÀ
country (nation)	國	ㄍㄨㄛˊ	国	GUÓ
cow (cattle)	牛	ㄋㄧㄡˊ	牛	NIÚ
cup (glass)	杯，杯子	ㄅㄟ, ㄅㄟ˙ㄗ	杯，杯子	BĒI, bēizi
daughter	女兒	ㄋㄩˇ ㄦ	女儿	NǙ ÉR
desk; table	桌，桌子	ㄓㄨㄛ, ㄓㄨㄛ˙ㄗ	桌，桌子	ZHUŌ, zhuōzi
dog	狗	ㄍㄡˇ	狗	GŎU
dot; spot	點	ㄉㄧㄢ	点	DIĂN

English meaning	Traditional	BoPoMoFo	Simplified	Pinyin
dragon	龍	ㄌㄨㄥˊ	龙	LÓNG
leather shoes	皮鞋	ㄆㄧˊ ㄒㄧㄝˊ	皮鞋	PÍ XIÉ
duck	鴨，鴨子	ㄧㄚ，ㄧㄚ·ㄗ	鸭，鸭子	YĀ, yāzi
duckling	小鴨子	ㄒㄧㄠˇ ㄧㄚ·ㄗ	小鸭子	XIǍO YĀZI
ear	耳	ㄦˇ	耳	ĚR
egg	蛋	ㄉㄢˋ	蛋	DÀN
eight	八	ㄅㄚ	八	BĀ
eleven	十一	ㄕˊ ㄧ	十一	SHÍ YĪ
father	爸，爸爸	ㄅㄚˋ，ㄅㄚ·ㄅㄚ	爸，爸爸	BÀ, bàba
female	女	ㄋㄩˇ	女	NǓ
field (farm with water)	田	ㄊㄧㄢˊ	田	TIÁN
fine (good, nice)	好	ㄏㄠˇ	好。	HǍO
fire	火	ㄏㄨㄛˇ	火	HUǑ
fish	魚	ㄩˊ	鱼	YÚ
five	五	ㄨˇ	五	WǓ
flower	花,花兒	ㄏㄨㄚ，ㄏㄨㄚ·ㄦ	花，花儿	HUĀ; HUĀR
foot	足	ㄗㄨˊ	足	ZÚ
fork	叉，叉子	ㄔㄚ，ㄔㄚ·ㄗ	叉，叉子	CHĀ, chāzi
four	四	ㄙˋ	四	SÌ
fruit	果，果子	ㄍㄨㄛˇ，ㄍㄨㄛˇ·ㄗ	果，果子	GUǑ, guǒzi
frog	蛙	ㄨㄚ	蛙	WĀ
fur	毛	ㄇㄠˊ	毛	MÁO

English meaning	Traditional	BoPoMoFo	Simplified	Pinyin
garlic	蒜	ㄙㄨㄢ	蒜	SUÀN
girl	女孩子	ㄋㄩ ㄏㄞ˙ㄗ	女孩子	NǙ HAÍZI
good (nice, fine)	好	ㄏㄠ	好	HǍO
good morning, early	早	ㄗㄠ	早	ZǍO
goodbye	再見	ㄗㄞ ㄐㄧㄢ	再见	ZÀI JIÀN
grass	草	ㄘㄠ	草	CǍO
hair	髮，頭髮	ㄈㄚ，ㄊㄡ˙ㄈㄚ	发，头发	FÀ; tóufa
he (him)	他	ㄊㄚ	他	TĀ
head	頭	ㄊㄡ	头	TÓU
heart	心	ㄒㄧㄣ	心	XĪN
heel (follow)	跟	ㄍㄣ	跟	GĒN
her (hers)	她的	ㄊㄚ˙ㄉㄜ	她的	TĀDE
his	他的	ㄊㄚ˙ㄉㄜ	他的	TĀDE
horse	馬	ㄇㄚ	马	MǍ
house	房，房子	ㄈㄤ，ㄈㄤ˙ㄗ	房，房子	FÁNG, fángzi
how	怎麼	ㄗㄣ˙ㄇㄜ	怎么	ZĚNME
how many	幾，幾個	ㄐㄧ，ㄐㄧ˙ㄍㄜ	几，几个	JǏ, jǐ ge?
I (me)	我	ㄨㄛ	我	WǑ
ice	冰	ㄅㄧㄥ	冰	BĪNG
ink	墨水	ㄇㄛ ㄕㄨㄟ	墨水	MÒ SHUǏ
ink stick	墨	ㄇㄛ	墨	MÒ
it	它	ㄊㄚ	它	TĀ
jade	玉	ㄩ	玉	YÙ

English meaning	Traditional	BoPoMoFo	Simplified	Pinyin
gelatin	凍	ㄉㄨㄥ	冻	DÒNG
kitten	小貓	ㄒㄧㄠ ㄇㄠ	小猫	XIǍO MĀO
knife	刀，刀子	ㄉㄠ，ㄉㄠ·ㄗ	刀，刀子	DĀO, dāozi
lamp	燈	ㄉㄥ	灯	DĒNG
leaf (leaves)	葉，葉子	ㄧㄝ，ㄧㄝ·ㄗ	叶，叶子	YÈ, yèzi
letters (mail)	信	ㄒㄧㄣ	信	XÌN
light; ray; beam	光	ㄍㄨㄤ	光	GUĀNG
little; small	小	ㄒㄧㄠ	小	XIǍO
male	男	ㄋㄢ	男	NÁN
man	人，男人	ㄖㄣ，ㄋㄢ ㄖㄣ	人，男人	RÉN, NÁNRÉN
meat	肉	ㄖㄡ	肉	RÒU
middle	中	ㄓㄨㄥ	中	ZHŌNG
milk	奶	ㄋㄞ	奶	NǍI
monkey	猴，猴子	ㄏㄡ，ㄏㄡ·ㄗ	猴，猴子	HÓU, hóuzi
moon	月	ㄩㄝ	月	YUÈ
moonlight	月光	ㄩㄝ ㄍㄨㄤ	月光	YUÈ GUĀNG
mother	媽、媽媽	ㄇㄚ，ㄇㄚ·ㄇㄚ	妈，妈妈	MĀ, māma
mouse (rat)	鼠	ㄕㄨ	鼠	SHǓ, laoshǔ
mouth	嘴	ㄗㄨㄟ	咀	ZUǏ
mud	泥	ㄋㄧ	泥	NÍ
my (mine)	我的	ㄨㄛ·ㄉㄜ	我的	WǑDE
name	名字	ㄇㄧㄥ ㄗ	名字	MÍNGZÌ

English meaning	Traditional	BoPoMoFo	Simplified	Pinyin
nest	窩	ㄨㄛ	窝	WŌ
new words	生字	ㄕㄥ ㄗ	生字	SHĒNG ZÌ
newspaper	報，報紙	ㄅㄠ，ㄅㄠˋ ㄓˇ	报，报纸	BÀO, baòzhǐ
nice (good, fine)	好	ㄏㄠˇ	好	HǍO
no, not	不	ㄅㄨˋ；ㄅㄨˊ	不	BÙ-; BÚ-
old	老	ㄌㄠˇ	老	LǍO
once	一次	ㄧˊ ㄘ	一次	YÍ CÌ
once more	再一次	ㄗㄞ ㄧˊ ㄘ	再一次	ZÀI YÍ CÌ
one	一	ㄧ	一	YĪ
onion	蔥	ㄘㄨㄥ	葱	CŌNG
opening; mouth	口	ㄎㄡˇ	口	KǑU
orange juice	橘子水	ㄐㄩˊ·ㄗ ㄕㄨㄟˇ	桔子水	JÚZI SHUǏ
our (ours)	我們的	ㄨㄛˇ·ㄇㄣ·ㄉㄜ	我们的	WǑMENDE
panda	熊貓	ㄒㄩㄥˊ ㄇㄠ	熊猫	XIÓNGMĀO
pants (trousers)	褲，褲子	ㄎㄨˋ，ㄎㄨˋ·ㄗ	裤，裤子	KÙ, kùzi
paper	紙	ㄓˇ	纸	ZHǏ
pear	梨	ㄌㄧˊ	梨	LÍ
pen	筆	ㄅㄧˇ	笔	BǏ
people (man)	人	ㄖㄣˊ	人	RÉN
phoenix	鳳	ㄈㄥˋ	凤	FÈNG
picture; painting	畫，畫兒	ㄏㄨㄚˋ，ㄏㄨㄚˋ·ㄦ	画，画儿	HUÀ; HUÀR
pig	豬	ㄓㄨ	猪	ZHŪ

English meaning	Traditional	BoPoMoFo	Simplified	Pinyin
pine	松	ㄙㄨㄥ	松	SŌNG
pistil	蕊	ㄖㄨㄟˇ	蕊	RUǏ
plate	盤，盤子	ㄆㄢˊ，ㄆㄢˊ·ㄗ	盘，盘子	PÁN, pánzi
plum	李，李子	ㄌㄧˇ，ㄌㄧˇ·ㄗ	李，李子	LǏ, lǐzi
puppy	小狗	ㄒㄧㄠˇ ㄍㄡˇ	小狗	XIǍO GǑU
rabbit	兔，兔子	ㄊㄨˋ，ㄊㄨˋ·ㄗ	兔，兔子	TÙ, tùzi
rain	雨	ㄩˇ	雨	YǓ
raincoat	雨衣	ㄩˇㄧ	雨衣	YǓ YĪ
raw; be born; strange ...	生	ㄕㄥ	生	SHĒNG
rocket	火箭	ㄏㄨㄛˇ ㄐㄧㄢˋ	火箭	HUǑ JIÀN
room	屋，屋子	ㄨ，ㄨ·ㄗ	屋，屋子	WŪ, wūzi
ruler	尺，尺子	ㄔˇ，ㄔˇ·ㄗ	尺，尺子	CHǏ, chǐzi
seed, child	子	ㄗ	子	ZǏ
seven	七	ㄑㄧ	七	QĪ
six	六	ㄌㄧㄡˋ	六	LIÙ
she (her)	她	ㄊㄚ	她	TĀ
shelf	架，架子	ㄐㄧㄚˋ，ㄐㄧㄚˋ·ㄗ	架，架子	JIÀ, jiàzi
shoes	鞋，鞋子	ㄒㄧㄝˊ，ㄒㄧㄝˊ·ㄗ	鞋，鞋子	XIÉ, xiézi
silk	絲	ㄙ	丝	SĪ
skin	皮	ㄆㄧˊ	皮	PÍ
skirt	裙，裙子	ㄑㄩㄣˊ，ㄑㄩㄣˊ·ㄗ	裙，裙子	QÚN, qúnzi
sky	天	ㄊㄧㄢ	天	TIĀN

English meaning	Traditional	BoPoMoFo	Simplified	Pinyin
small; little	小	ㄒㅣㄠˇ	小	XIǍO
snow	雪	ㄒㄩㄝˇ	ヨ	XUĚ
snowman	雪人	ㄒㄩㄝˇ ㄖㄣˊ	ヨ人	XUĚ RÉN
soccer	足球	ㄗㄨˊ ㄑㄧㄡˊ	足球	ZÚQIÚ
socks	襪 , 襪子	ㄨㄚˋ, ㄨㄚˋ·ㄗ	袜 , 袜子	WÀ, wàzi
son	兒 , 兒子	ㄦˊ , ㄦˊ·ㄗ	儿 , 儿子	ÉR, érzi
spark	火花	ㄏㄨㄛˇ ㄏㄨㄚ	火花	HUǑ HUĀ
spot; dot	點	ㄉㄧㄢˇ	点	DIǍN
star, stars	星 , 星星	ㄒㄧㄥ, ㄒㄧㄥ ㄒㄧㄥ	星 , 星星	XĪNG, xīngxīng
stick	棍 , 棍子	ㄍㄨㄣˋ, ㄍㄨㄣˋ·ㄗ	棍 , 棍子	GÙN, gùnzi
still	還	ㄏㄞˊ	还	HÁI-
student	學生	ㄒㄩㄝˊ ㄕㄥ	学生	XUÉSHĒNG
sun	日	ㄖˋ	日	RÌ
table; desk	桌 , 桌子	ㄓㄨㄛ, ㄓㄨㄛ·ㄗ	桌 , 桌子	ZHUŌ, zhuōzi
tangerine; orange	橘 , 橘子	ㄐㄩˊ , ㄐㄩˊ·ㄗ	桔 , 桔子	JÚ, júzi
teacher; master	師 , 老師	ㄕ , ㄌㄠˇ ㄕ	师 , 老师	SHĪ, lǎoshī
ten	十	ㄕˊ	十	SHÍ
that	那	ㄋㄚˋ, ㄋㄟˋ	那	NÀ, NÈI
their; theirs	他們的	ㄊㄚ·ㄇㄣ·ㄉㄜ	他们的	TĀMENDE
they; them	他們	ㄊㄚ·ㄇㄣ	他们	TĀMEN
this	這	ㄓㄜˋ, ㄓㄟˋ	这	ZHÈ; ZHÈI
thorn	刺	ㄘˋ	刺	CÌ
three	三	ㄙㄢ	三	SĀN

English meaning	Traditional	BoPoMoFo	Simplified	Pinyin
to be (am, are, is was, were)	是	ㄕ	是	SHÌ
to be in/on/at/under) ...	在	ㄗㄞ	在	ZÀI
to call	叫	ㄐㄧㄠ	叫	JIÀO
to draw	畫	ㄏㄨㄚ	画	HUÀ
to give	給	ㄍㄟ	给	GĚI
to have	有	ㄧㄡ	有	YǑU
to have not	沒有	ㄇㄟ·ㄧㄡ	没有	MÉIYOU
to hear; listen	聽	ㄊㄧㄥ	听	TĪNG
to know how; can	會	ㄏㄨㄟ	会	HUÌ
to learn	學	ㄒㄩㄝ	学	XUÉ
to read	念	ㄋㄧㄢ	念	NIÀN
to see; to look, to watch	看	ㄎㄢ	看	KÀN
to sing	唱	ㄔㄤ	唱	CHÀNG
to speak; to say, to talk	說	ㄕㄨㄛ	说	SHUŌ
to thank	謝，謝謝	ㄒㄧㄝ，ㄒㄧㄝ·ㄒㄧㄝ	谢，谢谢	XIÈ, xiexie
to understand	懂	ㄉㄨㄥ	懂	DǑNG
to want	要	ㄧㄠ	要	YÀO
to write	寫	ㄒㄧㄝ	写	XIĚ
together	一起	ㄧ ㄑㄧ	一起	YÌ QǏ
together with	跟⋯一起	ㄍㄣ⋯⋯ㄧ ㄑㄧ	跟⋯一起	GĒN ... YÌQǏ
train	火車	ㄏㄨㄛ ㄔㄜ	火车	HUǑ CHĒ
tree	樹	ㄕㄨ	树	SHÙ

English meaning	Traditional	BoPoMoFo	Simplified	Pinyin
turkey	火鷄	ㄏㄨㄛˇ ㄐㄧ	火鸡	HUǑ JĪ
twelve	十二	ㄕˊ ㄦˋ	十二	SHÍ ÈR
two	二	ㄦˋ	二	ÈR
two of	兩，兩個	ㄌㄧㄤˇ, ㄌㄧㄤˇ·ㄍㄜ	两，两个	LIǍNG, liǎng ge
umbrella	傘	ㄙㄢˇ	伞	SǍN
United States	美國	ㄇㄟˇ ㄍㄨㄛˊ	美国	MĚIGUÓ
vegetable; dishes (food)	菜	ㄘㄞˋ	菜	CÀI
very	很	ㄏㄣˇ	很	HĚN-
wall	牆	ㄑㄧㄤˊ	墙	QIÁNG
water	水	ㄕㄨㄟˇ	水	SHUǏ
we (us)	我們	ㄨㄛˇ·ㄇㄣ	我们	WǑMEN
what	甚麼	ㄕㄣˊ·ㄇㄜ	什么	SHÉNME
which, which one	哪，哪個	ㄋㄚˇ, ㄋㄚˇ·ㄍㄜ ㄋㄟˇ, ㄋㄟˇ·ㄍㄜ	哪，哪个	NǍ, nǎ ge NĚI, něi ge
white	白	ㄅㄞˊ	白	BÁI
who (whom)	誰	ㄕㄨㄟˊ; ㄕㄟˊ	谁	SHUÍ; SHÉI
language	話	ㄏㄨㄚˋ	话	HUÀ
whose	誰的	ㄕㄨㄟˊ·ㄉㄜ; ㄕㄟˊ·ㄉㄜ	谁的	SHUÍDE; SHÉIDE
wind	風	ㄈㄥ	风	FĒNG
woman	女人	ㄋㄩˇ ㄖㄣˊ	女人	NǙ RÉN
yes	是	ㄕˋ	是	SHÌ
you	你、您，你們	ㄋㄧˇ, ㄋㄧㄣˊ; ㄋㄧˇ·ㄇㄣ	你、您，你们	NǏ, NÍN (singular); NǏMEN (plural)
your (yours)	你們的 你的 您的	ㄋㄧˇ·ㄇㄣ·ㄉㄜ ㄋㄧˇ·ㄉㄜ, ㄋㄧㄣˊ·ㄉㄜ	你们的	NǏMENDE (plural) NǏDE; NÍNDE (singular)

English meaning	Traditional	BoPoMoFo	Simplified	Pinyin
to be (am, are, is was, were)	是	ㄕˋ	是	SHÌ
to be in/on/at/ under) ...	在	ㄗㄞˋ	在	ZÀI
to call	叫	ㄐㄧㄠˋ	叫	JIÀO
to draw	畫	ㄏㄨㄚˋ	画	HUÀ
to give	給	ㄍㄟˇ	给	GĚI
to have	有	ㄧㄡˇ	有	YǑU
to have not	沒有	ㄇㄟˊㄧㄡ	没有	MÉIYOU
to hear; listen	聽	ㄊㄧㄥ	听	TĪNG
to know how; can	會	ㄏㄨㄟˋ	会	HUÌ
to learn	學	ㄒㄩㄝˊ	学	XUÉ
to read	念	ㄋㄧㄢˋ	念	NIÀN
to see; to look, to watch	看	ㄎㄢˋ	看	KÀN
to sing	唱	ㄔㄤˋ	唱	CHÀNG
to speak; to say, to talk	說	ㄕㄨㄛ	说	SHUŌ
to thank	謝，謝謝	ㄒㄧㄝˋ, ㄒㄧㄝˋㄒㄧㄝ	谢，谢谢	XIÈ, xìexie
to understand	懂	ㄉㄨㄥˇ	懂	DǑNG
to want	要	ㄧㄠˋ	要	YÀO
to write	寫	ㄒㄧㄝˇ	写	XIĚ
together	一起	ㄧˋㄑㄧˇ	一起	YÌ QǏ
together with	跟⋯一起	ㄍㄣ⋯⋯ㄧˋㄑㄧˇ	跟⋯一起	GĒN ... YÌQǏ
train	火車	ㄏㄨㄛˇ ㄔㄜ	火车	HUǑ CHĒ
tree	樹	ㄕㄨˋ	树	SHÙ

English meaning	Traditional	BoPoMoFo	Simplified	Pinyin
turkey	火鷄	ㄏㄨㄛ ㄐㄧ	火鸡	HUǑ JĪ
twelve	十二	ㄕ ㄦ	十二	SHÍ ÈR
two	二	ㄦ	二	ÈR
two of	兩，兩個	ㄌㄧㄤ，ㄌㄧㄤ·ㄍㄜ	两，两个	LIǍNG，liǎng ge
umbrella	傘	ㄙㄢ	伞	SǍN
United States	美國	ㄇㄟ ㄍㄨㄛ	美国	MĚIGUÓ
vegetable; dishes (food)	菜	ㄘㄞ	菜	CÀI
very	很	ㄏㄣ	很	HĚN-
wall	牆	ㄑㄧㄤ	墙	QIÁNG
water	水	ㄕㄨㄟ	水	SHUǏ
we (us)	我們	ㄨㄛ·ㄇㄣ	我们	WǑMEN
what	甚麼	ㄕㄣ·ㄇㄜ	什么	SHÉNME
which, which one	哪，哪個	ㄋㄚ，ㄋㄚ·ㄍㄜ ㄋㄟ，ㄋㄟ·ㄍㄜ	哪，哪个	NǍ，nǎ ge NĚI，něi ge
white	白	ㄅㄞ	白	BÁI
who (whom)	誰	ㄕㄨㄟ；ㄕㄟ	谁	SHUÍ；SHÉI
language	話	ㄏㄨㄚ	话	HUÀ
whose	誰的	ㄕㄨㄟ·ㄉㄜ；ㄕㄟ·ㄉㄜ	谁的	SHUÍDE；SHÉIDE
wind	風	ㄈㄥ	风	FĒNG
woman	女人	ㄋㄩ ㄖㄣ	女人	NǙ RÉN
yes	是	ㄕ	是	SHÌ
you	你，您，你們	ㄋㄧ，ㄋㄧㄣ；ㄋㄧ·ㄇㄣ	你、您，你们	NǏ，NÍN (singular); NǏMEN (plural)
your (yours)	你們的 你的 您的	ㄋㄧ·ㄇㄣ·ㄉㄜ ㄋㄧ·ㄉㄜ，ㄋㄧㄣ·ㄉㄜ	你们的	NǏMENDE (plural) NǏDE；NÍNDE (singular)